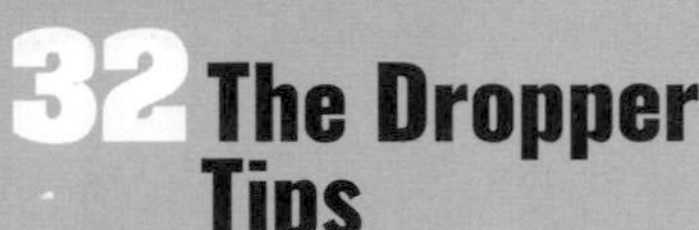

Published 2021
Little Brother Books Ltd, Ground Floor, 23 Southernhay East, Exeter, Devon, EX1 1QL

Printed in Poland. ul. Połczyńska 99,01303 Warszawa

books@littlebrotherbooks.co.uk
www.littlebrotherbooks.co.uk

Contributions from: Simon Brew, Claire Brunton, James Hunt, John Moore, Laura Pelham, Rory Reynolds, Rachel Storry, Thomas Brew, Isabel Brew, Emmy Hunt.

WELCOME!

Hello and welcome! If you're holding this book, we reckon you love Roblox just as much as we do, and we're going to have loads of fun exploring it over the coming pages!

To kick off, we'll look at the story behind Roblox and how it came to exist, sharing tonnes of amazing facts along the way too. You'll also find masses of tips for the many different games you can play within Roblox. As there are so many to choose from, we've picked our favourites, and we think they might be ones you love too!

Of course, Roblox is changing all the time, so chances are it will be even more awesome by the time you read these words.

Enjoy your Robloxing!

ROBLOX

Lantern

PICK YOUR AVATAR

There's no better place to start with Roblox than by coming up with an epic avatar for your character. If you haven't already done this, pick the 'Avatar' option from the list on the main menu screen of Roblox. Here you'll see your current avatar, plus loads of options for different clothes, animations, costumes and body types. Many of these are available for free, but some options do come with a price.

It's heaps of fun picking your avatar, and well worth taking the time to come up with something fantastic!

ROBLOX STUDIO

GET CREATIVE

Don't forget that one of the best things about Roblox is you can make your own stuff!

MAKE YOUR OWN GAME

GET MAKING

Don't forget that one of the best things about Roblox is you can make your own stuff! If you click on the 'Create' option, you'll be taken to Roblox Studio, where you can start work on your own games, objects and such like. It takes a little while to set up the first time you use it, and it can seem a bit overwhelming, but it's definitely worth giving it a go – perhaps start by making your own obby game?!

THE STORY OF ROBLOX!

How did Roblox come about in the first place? Well, it turns out that the idea for the game is nearly 20 years old!

The games that we play on our computers, phones, tablets and games consoles are made by talented people with ambitious ideas – but they can take years to create! This was certainly the case with Roblox!

The brainboxes behind Roblox are David Baszucki and Erik Cassel, and they first started working on it all the way back in the year 2003. Even then, it took some time before they were happy to release it properly, and the first version came out in 2006. Unusually, it has continued to evolve ever since!

BRAINS

David used to work at Knowledge Revolution, which he set up himself in 1989. It was a company that released educational software which taught people physics. When Erik read about the company, he wanted to work for it. Impressed by his talent, David hired him and the pair also became good friends. When Knowledge Revolution was bought by another company in 1999, they continued to work together.

The two programmers loved physics and they believed they could turn their passion into a game for youngsters. They were going to call it Dynablock, but decided Roblox sounded better. We can't help but agree with them there!

To make the game, they needed to work for many hours each day in an office in Menlo Park, California, over in America. In 2004, a small number of players were invited to try an early test version, known as a beta. More people were allowed to try it the following year.

Lots of people began to learn the Lua scripting language to see what they could make

PLAYTIME

At this time, players couldn't make their own games using Roblox. David and Erik decided to add that feature in 2006, when they allowed everybody to release the first official version of Roblox!

Lots of people soon began to learn the Lua scripting language to see what they could make. Some worked on a small map called Forest of Desolation, and there was a popular game called Sunset Plain, one of the first to use the BrickBattle game mode. You can still play some of these games today. Why not check out Experience Gravity?

By now, the team of people making Roblox had grown. Many people who had worked with the pair before at their old companies joined David and Erik and helped to make the online game platform even better. They also decided that players should be able to communicate with each other in the game, so a private messaging feature was added. To ensure everyone under the age of 13 was safe online (which is very important), a Safe Chat feature was introduced.

NEW FEATURES

Roblox has, of course, grown considerably over the years, and a new premium version was released in 2007. Called the Builders Club, it gave users a daily income of R$15 – a Roblox currency – as well as the ability to create personal servers, join up to 10 groups and make up to 10 places active. Users could even sell clothes, receive a badge and get a hard hat. By giving users the tools they needed, Roblox unleashed their creativity to such a level that the team who made the game creation system were amazed. That wonderful user creativity has been at the heart of Roblox every since.

FUN

In 2010, Erik recalled the day Roblox released its first multiplayer game with characters. He said 20 kids got together in the game Crossroads and began to build platforms on their characters' shoulders to carry each other around. "It was completely unexpected, collaborative and fun," he said.

People working for Roblox were also encouraged to experiment, and during a 'Hack Week' in 2011 they could work on any Roblox project they wished to improve.

Over time, Roblox was released on lots of different devices: iPad and iPhone in 2012, Android tablet and phone in 2014, and Xbox One in 2015. Games also became smoother in 2015 when Smooth Terrain was added, allowing players to use more realistic-looking grass, sand,

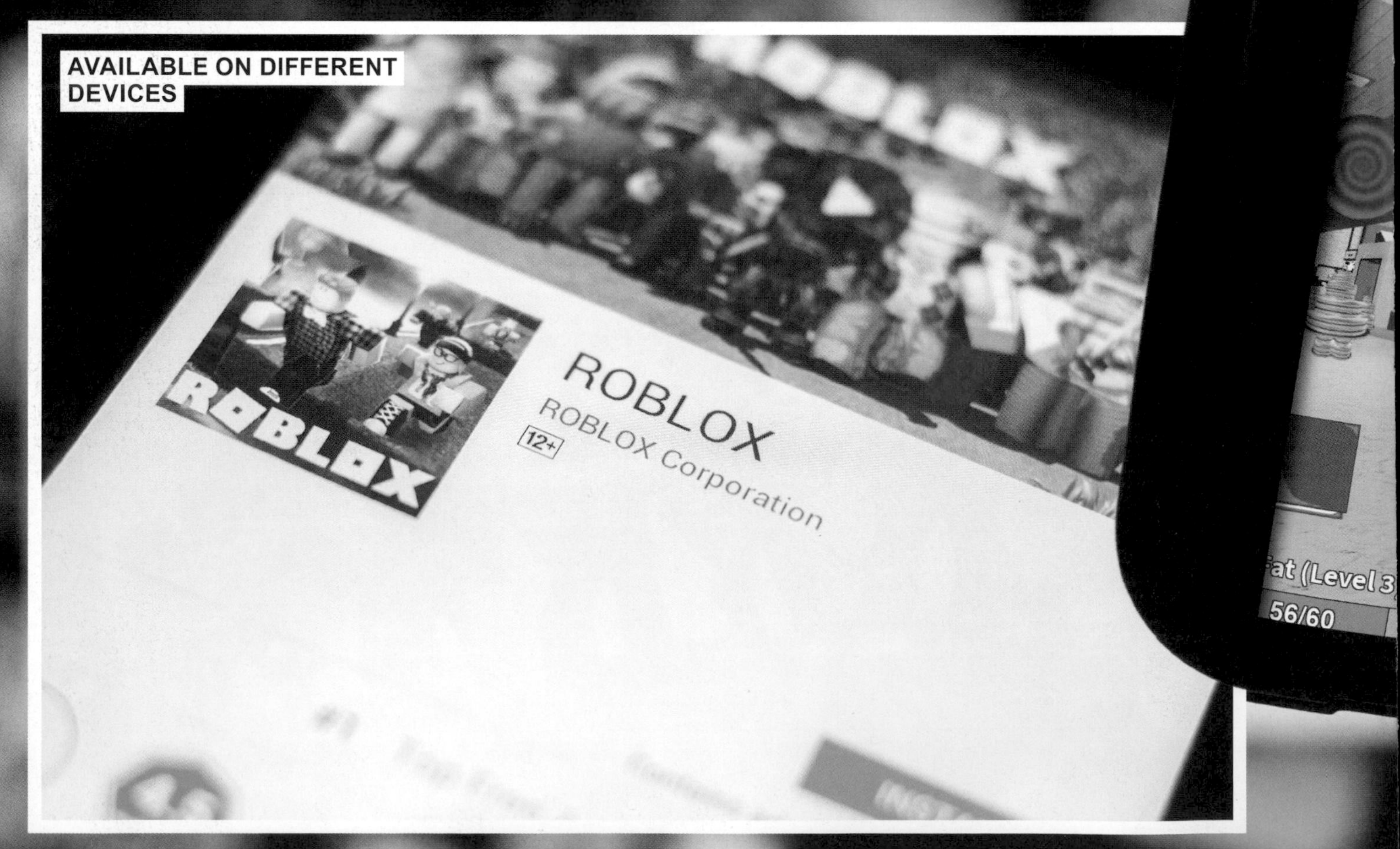

AVAILABLE ON DIFFERENT DEVICES

brick and rock in their creations. A virtual reality version was even created for the Oculus Rift headset in 2016. Roblox's creators wanted players to feel like they were in a massive interactive amusement park, and we think they managed to do just that!

It was around this time that Roblox saw a huge rise in popularity. Safe Chat was replaced with a new system that included an allowlist of words for under 13s and a denylist of words for those who were older. Users could also gather together thanks to a feature called Party Place and host virtual events.

With more than 164 million active users a month, Roblox certainly looks to have a strong future ahead of it!

Smooth Terrain allows players to use more realistic-looking grass, sand, brick and rock in their creations

TOWER OF HELL Hints & Tips

It's super-hard and super-fun – it's the Tower of Hell obby!

WELCOME TO THE TOWER

In this game, the objective is simple: across several modes, you and some other players have to safely climb the tower of hell without failing the randomised obby (a 'section') that changes every few minutes. If you do fail, it's back to the start. Whoever gets the furthest up or down the tower wins. Sounds easy, right?

SECRET SECTIONS

There are around 20 'secret sections' in Tower of Hell, which are roughly 20 times less likely to turn up than a normal section. They're normally grey in colour and look totally different from the other sections. Only one of these secret sections – the House – has any kill parts.

TRAILS

If you succeed in beating any sections, you can earn points to buy mutators or trails. Trails don't affect your abilities in the game – they're just for appearance. However, they DO show everyone how awesome you are at climbing! You'll get a few points every time you climb into a new section, and they stack up the more you play. If you look at the height indicator on the right, you'll see where and when you collected points, as well as where every other player is!

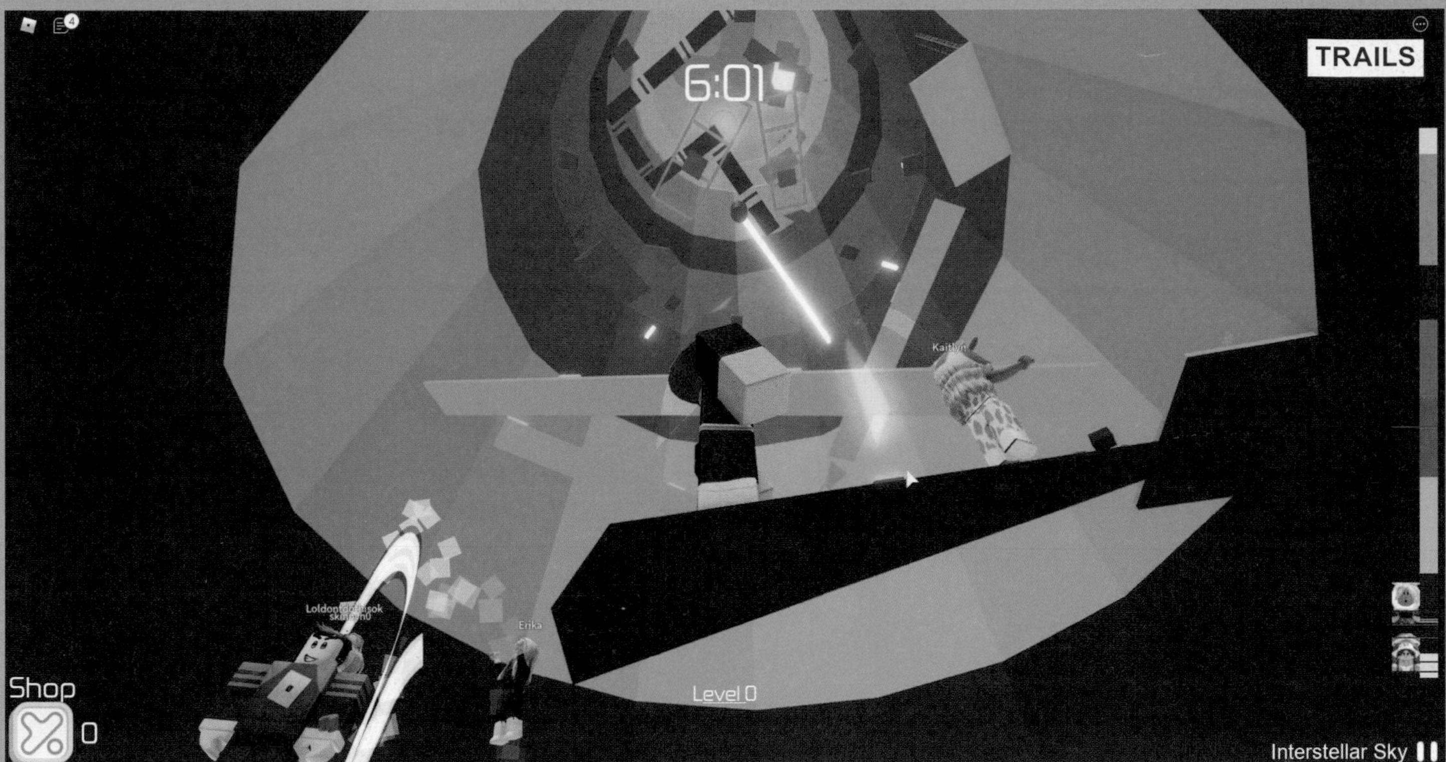

EXPERT TIPS

Descending the Tower is pretty tough! Here are some expert tips:

» **Ignore the timer.** Descending at a slow and steady pace gives you the best chance of success. If you rush, you're only likely to make a mistake!

» **Watch other players.** If you're not sure where to go, stand at the base and watch other players descend. This will help you see where the shortcuts are and the best way to get down.

» **Practise a lot.** Tonnes of random obbies come up, but the more you practise, the better you'll get.

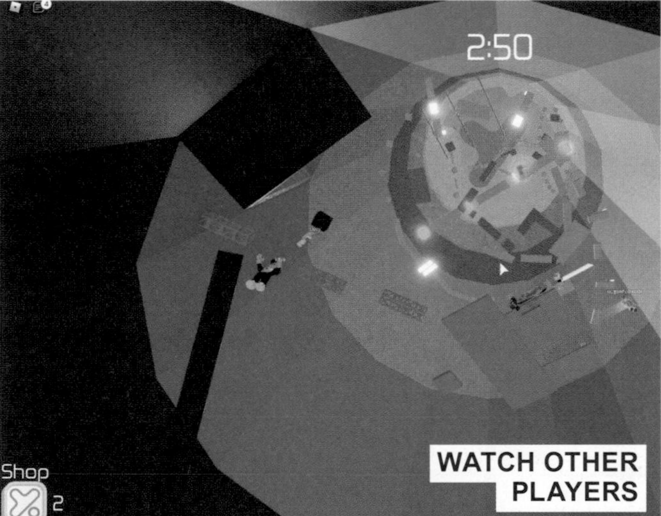

WATCH OTHER PLAYERS

AVOID MUTATORS

Plus, you'll start to see the same ones turn up again and again, which makes things easier!

» **Look for shortcuts.** It's often possible to skip parts of an obby, so test your luck when you play and try to remember which shortcuts work, and which only LOOK possible.

» **Avoid mutators.** Mutators change the gameplay, and there are nine overall. Although Low Gravity and Invincibility are pretty good, Negative, Foggy and Extra Time aren't much help to anyone, and High Speed can make things difficult too! You're better off sticking with the normal physics and trying not to adapt how you play.

ADOPT ME! Tips & Hints

How to master Roblox's popular pet-adoption simulator!

COLLECTING FREE MONEY

The best way to get money in Adopt Me! is to collect the login rewards. If you log in every day, you'll get money every day, plus big rewards on the 5th, 10th and 15th days before it resets. You don't have to do anything else – just log in!

GETTING EXTRA CASH

If you play as a baby in Adopt Me!, you get double the tasks – some for your pets and some for you – and every time you complete a task you get money. If you have friends who are playing, remember to form a family with them. That way, you'll earn bonus money when someone else completes a task.

USEFUL FURNITURE

Lots of furniture is decorative, but you can use some to complete tasks! Cribs allow you to complete the tired task. Pianos allow

If you play as a baby, you get double the tasks – some for your pets and some for you

TELEPORTING

you to complete the bored task. Water coolers and water bowls allow you to complete thirsty tasks. Food bowls and pizza dough/toppings allow you to complete the hungry task. Watch out for these items when you're decorating!

MONEY TREE

Consider buying a money tree. It will cost 1450 in-game dollars, but dispense 100 dollars every day, so after playing for 15 days it will start to pay for itself!

COLLECTING FREE MONEY

NEONS

To make a neon, you need to get four types of the same pet, level them up fully, then take them to a hidden cave, which you'll find under a bridge on Adoption Island. Here, you can swap your four pets for one neon pet. But beware – you can't ever swap them back!

TELEPORTING

To speed up travel around the island, you can teleport back to your home using Roblox's 'Reset character' option. You can also teleport straight to the gift shop using the 'Gifts' option in the inventory. Finally, you can get to the playground using the 'Strollers' option in the inventory, which teleports you to the stroller shop, just next to the playground!

A FREE LUNCH!

At the school, you can get a free apple from the desk found if you go left from the main entrance. This apple respawns, so you can collect it lots of times, if you remember! Other rooms in the school have free pet bowls filled with food and water, so you can feed your pet without using your own resources.

WHAT YOU NEED TO KNOW ABOUT ROBUX

You don't need Robux to enjoy Roblox, but there are advantages and disadvantages to the currency...

The in-game currency of Roblox is, of course, Robux. This is used to buy special upgrades in games and experiences, as well as extra abilities. Most games when you're playing Roblox will try to get you to buy something, but we'd always recommend being cautious, as the vast majority of games and experiences are perfectly enjoyable without spending any money, no matter what the game might be telling you.

SPENDING

If, of course, there's a game you really like or a creator you think is brilliant, you might want to support their work. That's what the Robux system is for, and one day maybe you'll make your own games and items that you'll want to sell for Robux yourself.

KEEP COUNT

You can always check exactly how many Robux you have in your account, because it's listed next to your account name on the main Roblox start screen. To top up, you can either buy a gift card from a real shop, or go online and buy Robux from the official Roblox store.

The vast majority of games and experiences are perfectly enjoyable without spending any money

BEWARE

Unfortunately, some people who use Roblox try to cheat and steal Robux from others. It's worth remembering the following, just to stay on the safe side:

» You can't officially earn free Robux from playing any of the games and experiences. If anyone says otherwise, be very wary.
» There are lots of scammers who claim they're giving away Robux on their websites. Avoid them!
» If you have Robux in your account, be absolutely sure you want to give some to others if that's what you're planning to do. It's always worth checking with a grown-up first.
» Always ask permission before buying something. Your grown-up may have left their payment details in Roblox by accident, and might not realise that you could build up a very big bill.

BUYING ROBUX

Note that the official Roblox store tries to encourage you to subscribe, so that you buy a set number of Robux every single month. Be absolutely sure that's something you want to do. You need to talk to your grown-up, as it might be better to make a one-off purchase in the first instance.

TAKE IT EASY

Remember, if you do get Robux in your account – and, again, it's perfectly fine if you don't! – spend them very carefully. Roblox makes it quite easy to buy lots of things and spend all your Robux very quickly. What's more, once they're spent, the company behind Roblox says you can't get them refunded, so you're not getting them back. There are loads of stories of people spending tonnes and tonnes of money without even realising it, because it's so easy to tap on something by accident and spend your Robux.

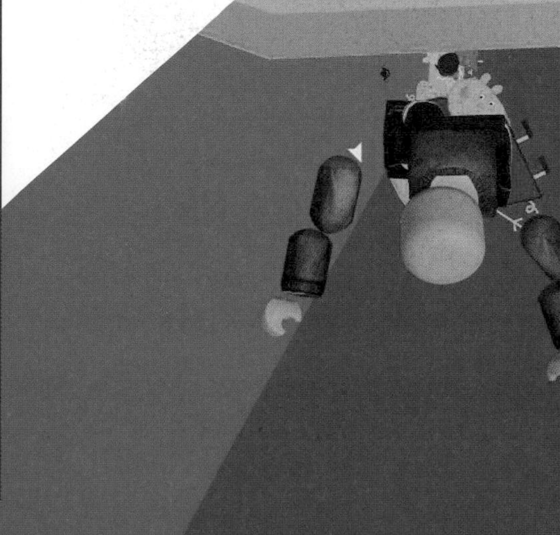

GET EATEN! ROBLOX'S YUCKIEST GAME!

Meet the Roblox game where the idea is simply to get eaten by something – and come out the other side!

Some Roblox games and experiences are warm and fuzzy. Some are scary and really challenging. Get Eaten! might just be the most horrible, though! Like many popular Roblox games, the idea behind it is really simple: you choose a piece of food to jump on, then try to get eaten.

It doesn't stop there, though. Should you manage to get eaten, you then pass through the insides of a Robloxian, come out of its bottom, and get flushed down the toilet (turning brown as you do). That's if everything goes to plan. Sometimes you might miss their mouth and go back to the start. At other times it may glitch. But basically, head for the slide, and once you're going down you don't need to move your controller until you get to the bottom…

CHOOSE YOUR FOOD

HOW ABOUT A CAR?!

Keep an eye out for hungry Robloxians, who'll have an alert above their head

WHAT DO I NEED TO DO?

This is basically a game of slides. You choose a piece of food that you want to be, then guide it towards one of the slides in the play arena. As usual with Roblox creations, most of the slides are locked at first, and you need to earn points to unlock them.

Keep an eye out for hungry Robloxians (the creatures at the bottom of the slides), who'll have an alert above their head and are worth aiming for. On the flip side, if a Robloxian is marked as either 'Full' or 'Throwing Up', avoid them for the time being. When they throw up, a whole lot of balls fire in your direction!

Ultimately, you only get points if you make it to the toilet at the very end. Those points are then used to unlock the other slides in the game, as well as vehicles and other food items. The harder slides to unlock inevitably earn you more points when you manage to make it to the bottom of them!

TAKE A SEAT!

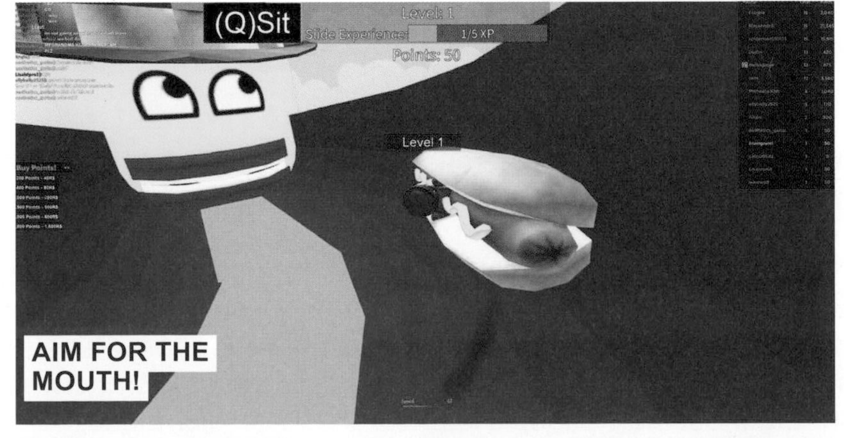

AIM FOR THE MOUTH!

ONE MORE THING

In the middle of the first play area, where you choose which slide to go down, there's also a beanstalk. Climb to the very top of this and you'll find a star. Go in the star, and you'll be taken upwards and find another slide! You'll need the points to unlock it first, though…

ROYALE HIGH Hints & tips

Collect diamonds and explore the world of Royale High, where school has never been such fun!

DAILY LOGIN

On Royale High, the daily login awards increase every day for 10 days. Log in every day in a row without missing any and you'll collect 12,000 diamonds, which is a fair amount for getting you started with some items from the outfit shop. Use diamonds to customise your outfits – there are loads of looks you can put together, and the rarest items require the most diamonds.

LEVELLING UP

Levelling up is the ideal way to get more diamonds, and to do that you need to collect XP, which you can do by attending classes. Remember that the longer you play, the more energy you expend – check your cellphone to view your energy levels. Go to sleep in your dorm room to get XP, and when you level up you'll get 300 free diamonds.

HALOS

LOOK OUT FOR SECRETS

Explore the map of Royale High and you'll find all sorts of cool secrets in every region of the game. Keep an eye out for diamonds, especially on the main campus. Remember you can fly to check out those hard-to-reach areas!

DRESSING UP

When you play Royale High, it's important to make sure the outfit you're wearing matches your mood, as other players will judge you based on how you look! If you're entering the pageants, try to keep your appearance on theme, so you can score more points and earn more diamonds by attracting the votes of your fellow entrants!

EVENTS

Royale High always has events themed around days of the calendar, such as Valentine's Day or Easter, and usually they'll add in map-exploration side quests, such as finding easter eggs or chests to open to get a reward. Look out for these events, and make sure you're familiar with the map so you can discover the hidden stuff quickly!

HALOS

Halos are some of the rarest items in Royale High. The easiest way to find them is to use the Fountain of Dreams in Divinia Park, where you can obtain one randomly. Around six new halos are made available each year and they usually coincide with in-game events. The fountain can only be used once every two hours, and you'll either win diamonds, lose diamonds, win random XP, have nothing happen or – very rarely – win a halo.

DRESSING UP

AMAZING ROBLOX NUMBERS!

Can you believe these amazing numerical facts about Roblox?!?

1997

When the first idea for Roblox was thought up, but there was still a long time before it was released.

OVER 40 MILLION

THE NUMBER OF DIFFERENT GAMES AVAILABLE TO PLAY IN ROBLOX – AND IT'S INCREASING EVERY MONTH!

50 MILLION
THE NUMBER OF NEW ROBLOX USERS REGISTERING DURING THE LOCKDOWN OF 2020

1 BILLION
THE FIRST ROBLOX GAME TO GET ONE BILLION VISITS WAS MEEPCITY, ALL THE WAY BACK IN 2016!

OVER 160 MILLION
The number of people playing Roblox every month!

2006
The year the first version of Roblox was released

75 BILLION
VIEWS OF ROBLOX VIDEOS ON YOUTUBE IN 2020 ALONE!

7 million
The number of people making games for Roblox!

OVER 30 MILLION
The number of people who log into Roblox EVERY DAY!

2007
The year the Robux currency was added to Roblox

OVER 23 BILLION!
THE NUMBER OF TIMES ADOPT ME! HAS BEEN LOADED UP

MAKE A CHARACTER!

Have you ever tried to draw a Robloxian of your own? We've made it easier: just copy the picture on the left into the space on the right, using the grid to break it down. Then you can customise it, and perhaps design a whole new avatar!

JAILBREAK Hints & Tips

Whether you want to try breaking out of jail or catch those who do, this cops & robbers roleplay is one of Roblox's crown jewels

THE GAME

If you play as a prisoner, you start Jailbreak by breaking out of prison in a number of different ways. Your next goal is to explore the rest of the map and commit heists to make cash. Meanwhile, if you play as the police, you'll be given weapons and vehicles to try to stop the robbers and get them back in jail!

KEY LOCATIONS

» **The Prison** – Where you can practise escaping and learn how to evade the cops!
» **The Apartments** – Get enough money and you can buy an apartment, which is the only place prisoners are safe from being arrested.
» **The Gun Shop** – Here you can buy rare weapons and do some shooting practice!

HEISTS TO LOOK OUT FOR

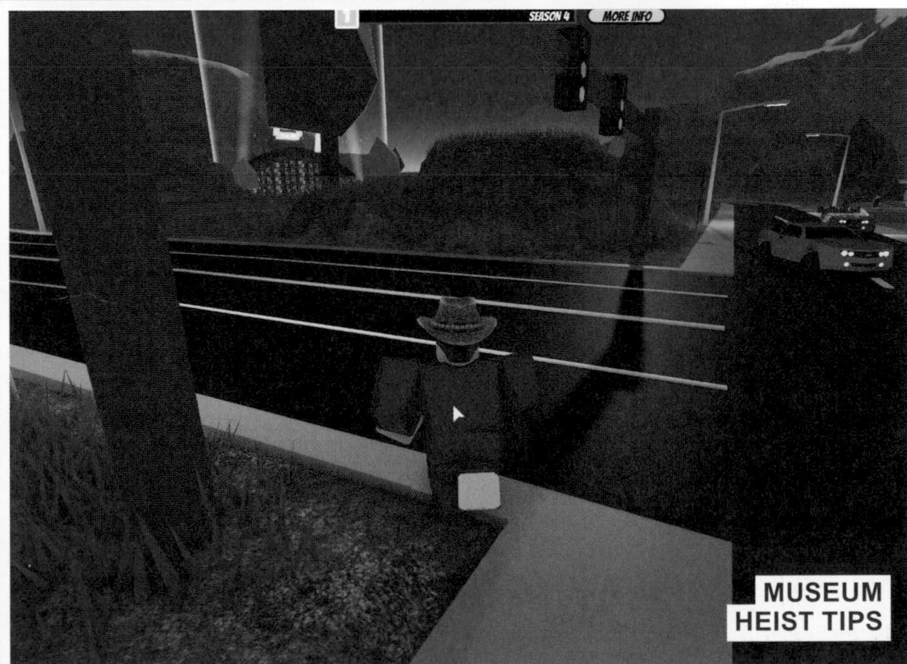

MUSEUM HEIST TIPS

HEISTS TO LOOK OUT FOR

There are nine main heists in Jailbreak – Bank, Cargo Ship, Cargo Train, Cash Truck, Jewelry Store, Museum, Passenger Train, Power Plant and Tomb. See if you can find them all! Cash Truck is the best – it only starts once 20 arrests have been made, but robbing it can earn you up to $13,200!

MUSEUM HEIST TIPS

The museum heist is relatively easy and lucrative, so here are some tips for getting it done faster:

» You can stand on the T-Rex pedestal to heal, as the security cameras can't see you there.

» Holding the museum bag on your back stops you from ragdolling, so you can jump off the museum roof and escape!

» Collecting an item while holding the bag makes it disappear, so avoid doing that!

» The most you can earn from robbing the museum without any boosts or assists is $3,500. If you have a Tier 4 Bigger Duffel Bag and a VIP gamepass, you can earn up to $8,400!

EASTER EGGS

Here are some of the best Jailbreak easter eggs:

» If you turn right before the town tunnel, you'll see a waterfall – behind it is an empty cave sometimes used for events (but also a great hiding place!).

» If you play the game between 9:30pm and 11:45pm (in-game), Piggy (from the game of the same name) will spawn in the sewers. If they kill you, you'll get Piggy Rims for your vehicle.

» If you search near Cheater Island, you can find four apples hidden underwater.

» If you fall into the volcano, you'll hear the sound of Darth Vader shouting "noooo!" from the *Star Wars* movies.

ROVILLE

IDEAS AND ADVICE

Jump into the world of RoVille, and you'll find a whole new life for your character!

One of the more popular games on Roblox, RoVille is a life-simulation game where your character can build their dream home, go to school, get a job and socialise with other players. It can be a whole lot of fun!

IN THE OFFICE!

GETTING STARTED

It pays to remember the basics and look after yourself properly in this game! Make sure your character keeps up their energy levels, their personal hygiene and their hunger. This will put them in a better mood, and you might even get promoted quicker! Just keep an eye on the gauges that appear on the left-hand side of the screen.

Fortunately, your home has everything you need. Just make sure you shower regularly, get enough sleep in your bed, and use your kitchen to cook yourself some food from time to time.

HOME COMFORTS

When it comes to your home in RoVille, you have a couple of options. Tap on the house icon on the little toolbar, and you have the choice of going into build mode or heading to the marketplace. In build mode, you can design and make your own house, whereas

in the marketplace you can buy a ready-built house, assuming you have enough funds, of course.

Don't just walk into other people's homes, though: they can simply ban you, and you'll quickly find yourself back outside!

WORKING FOR A LIVING

You can go to school or find a job in RoVille. Getting a job allows you to earn money, and the more hours you work and the more skilled you become at your job, the more cash you'll earn to spend on your home, for instance. Different jobs are done at different times of the day – don't expect too many people to be in school at three in the morning, for example! .

OTHER ADDITIONS

RoVille also lets you buy a pet (although be careful, because we found that some of them can glitch). You can also buy yourself a car, which makes it much quicker to get around the place. Don't forget – as if you could! – that you're able to customise loads of stuff too, including your car. Oh, and remember to jump in the driver's seat if you want to move your vehicle. In any other seat, you're only going to be a passenger!

HIDE & SEEK EXTREME TIPS

Roblox has featured hide and seek games for a very long time, but one of the best is Hide And Seek Extreme...

HOW TO PLAY

Hide And Seek Extreme is as simple as it sounds. One player is the seeker, and everyone else is a hider. The hiders hide, the seeker seeks – simply, right?!

Well, just to put a bit of a twist on it, the seeker is called 'It' – and if you're the It character, you get an extra power to help you catch the others. Maps are chosen randomly, and each one comes with plenty of nooks and crannies to explore. It might take you a few rounds to get used to a particular map, but it's worth learning as much as you can about it.

COMING, READY OR NOT

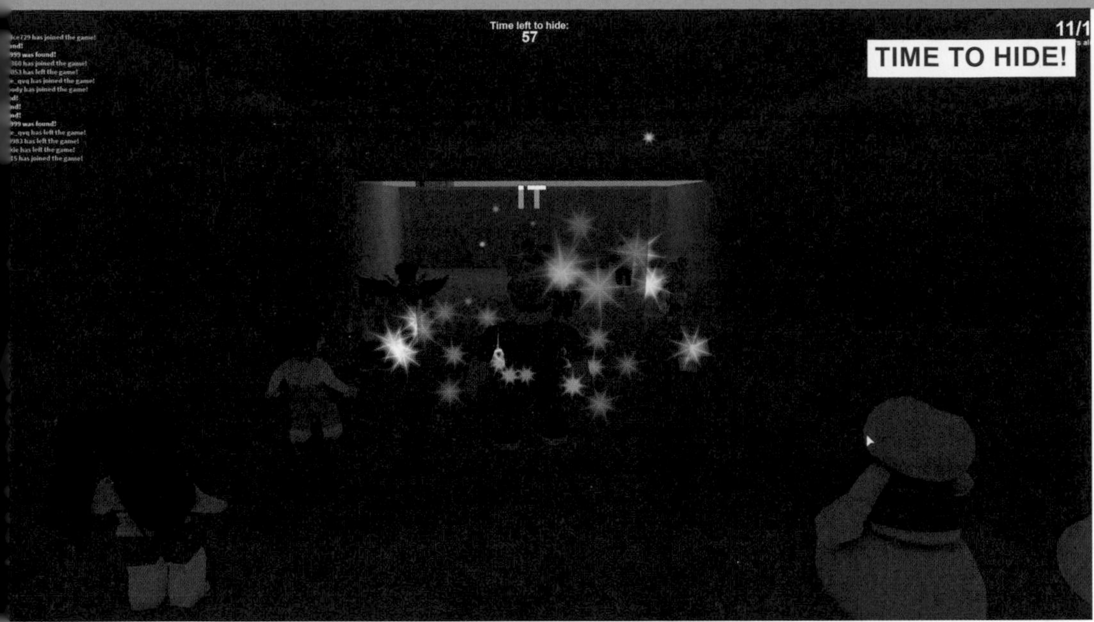

TIME TO HIDE!

AVOID HIGH HIDING PLACES

THE CLOCK IS TICKING

HIDING

Each play area tends to have a secret hiding spot or two, or a little feature that might help you get somewhere different on the map. Look out for teleporters or jump pads, for instance. In the level Ethan's Bedroom, there's a teleporter that can get you on top of the bunk bed in the room (you'll find it in the open drawer). It's also best to stop moving around once you've found a place to hide, as it's much easier to be seen if you're moving.

As a good rule of thumb, higher places are harder to reach (but that tends to be where people start looking for others first).

Also, pay attention to the bit on the screen that tells you how many studs away they are from you (effectively how many spaces). When that gets to under 100, they're really close. Stay as still as you can! The one exception to this is if you're certain you've been spotted – in which case, you may as well make a run for it. If time is nearly up, you might just survive.

One more thing: when you're caught, you go into Spectating Mode, where you can see every other player on the map. It's really useful for finding good hiding place tips!

SEEKING

If you're It, there's one instant advantage and one instant disadvantage. On the plus side, you can move a bit quicker than everyone else. On the downside, you start the game frozen, and everyone else gets some time to hide. Plus, every other player knows how far away you are from them.

This is where your special powers come in. In each round, you'll be able to place down a bit of glue (which sticks hiders to the spot who touch it for a few seconds), put down cameras (really useful), sprint (even more useful!) or, if you've been given the Yeti outfit, you might get a stun ability. With this, you hit the ground with a club and it stuns hiders who are running away!

HOW TO PLAY MURDER MYSTERY 2

This one's a large group mystery, as one of your fellow players is secretly a murderer! Gulp!

FIND THE MURDERER

Up to 12 people can play at once, so it can get a bit frantic! There are two weapons in the game – the murderer's knife and the sheriff's gun – but you can find loads of different versions by unboxing crates and spending coins.

TAKING PART

There are three roles in the game, and each player

ABOUT THE GAME

With this one, you need to choose from three different modes of play: Casual, Hardcore and Assassin. Those titles should give you a clue as to which is the easiest and which is the hardest!

You can play in at least 14 different maps, such as hospitals and offices. New ones are added regularly, but it means old ones disappear and become unplayable.

PICK YOUR GAME MODE

MAKE SURE YOU HIDE

You're an innocent? Run and hide! It's a giant game of hide and seek

is assigned one at random: murderer, sheriff or innocent.

OR KILL OTHER PLAYERS

If you're the murderer, you have to kill as many of the other players as possible before the time runs out. Be careful, though, as you don't want to get caught in the act, or the other players could kill you and you'll lose the game. Walk slowly, and don't hang out in large groups. You want to face people one on one so they can't identify you in the chat!

If you're the sheriff, it's your job to find and shoot the murderer. Take your time, because if you kill an innocent you'll die and be out of the game. You also don't want to be mistaken for the murderer!

CHOOSE YOUR MAP

You're an innocent? Run and hide! It's a giant game of hide and seek. You might think it's a good idea to follow others, but they may think you're the killer, so it's every person for themselves! Use objects like doors to hide behind, or climb on top of items – passers-by might miss you and you can see who's coming!

If the sheriff is killed, they'll drop their gun. An innocent can then pick it up and try to identify the murderer.

THE DROPPER TIPS

This game is all about falling to the flashing box on the floor, but if only it were that easy!

DON'T HIT THE TREES

One thing the creators of The Dropper are keen to stress is that ALL levels of the game are possible. There are, after all, some Roblox games that glitch and don't let you finish every stage. That's not the case with this one, though!

The idea is simple: you drop down a big hole, and you need to reach the bottom without hitting any obstacles. In the early levels, that's really easy. In the later levels? Er, it gets much more tricky!

Lots of the levels are really funny, and you might recognise that many have been influenced by TV shows and films.

PLAYING TIPS

This game takes a bit of getting used to, and you're likely to need several attempts at many of the levels once you're past the very simple ones. It's quite easy to get annoyed and start shouting at your screen!

Two things will really help you, though. First, quickly get used to how fast your character

ONE FOR FOOTIE FANS

can move. Whilst they plummet to the floor at speed, they don't move with the same urgency up, down, left and right.

Next, you need to be watching closely. You can see the majority of obstacles you're going to be coming up against from some way off. It gets really hard when the gaps become smaller and those obstacles are packed closer together, but take a second at the start of each level to have a good look around.

It's also worth varying your jump-off point. At first, you might just run towards the hole in the ground and simply fall in, but you can also jump in at the sides, or jump to the far side of the hole. Don't just assume that you always have to start from the very same place!

Be wary too of just going to the sides of levels. With some of the drops, if you hit the sides, it's game over!

You can use Robux to skip a level if you get totally stuck, but going back to what we said at the start, every level IS possible. Past level 100, though, they become very, very tricky!

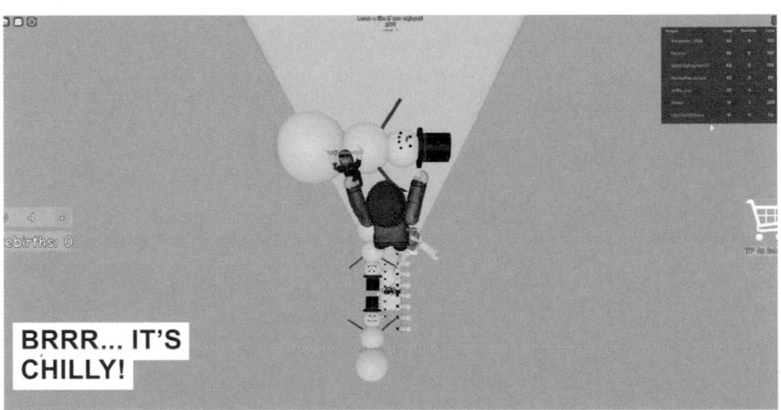
BRRR... IT'S CHILLY!

CHOOSE YOUR LEVEL

ONE MORE THING

One thing we love about The Dropper is the wide range of music that changes with the theme of each of the levels. Some of the accompanying tunes and sounds are hilarious!

PIGGY Hints & Tips

One of the most popular survival horror games on Roblox, here's how to survive – or how to catch other players!

PLAYER TIPS

» Remember Piggy can't kill two people in quick succession. If you're with someone and they get killed, you should be able to rush past Piggy without getting caught.

» Bots will never walk off the side of stairs, so if you're being chased you can use that behaviour to take shortcuts where you won't be followed.

» If Piggy is stunned, set off some of their traps, then they won't be able to come and get you.

» If Piggy is camping by the exit, use the time to collect ranged weapons and ammo, then shoot them so you can dash past.

THE PHOTO IS UNDER THE PURPLE CAR

PIGGY & TRAITOR TIPS

» If a map has NPCs (non-player characters), try to put traps near them so players have to sneak around them to interact with the NPCs.
» Traps can be placed in mid-air, so put them on the way down in tight or blind drops to catch people unawares.
» When chasing a player, remember you can sometimes close a door in front of them even if you're behind them.
» If you're a traitor, wait until the first player dies, then tell the other players they were the traitor!

HOW TO GET PIGGY'S TRUE ENDING

To get the true ending of Piggy, you have to complete the following steps:

» Collect all 13 Piggy badges by completing every map. You get a badge every time you complete a map, including one for both the good and bad endings for Plant (Chapter 12).

» Play City (Chapter 9) in Player + Bot mode, and complete the map while carrying Mrs. P's photo. You can find the photo underneath a purple, rusted car. It's hard to swing the camera into the right spot, so it will probably take you a few goes! Make sure you open the exit first, otherwise you won't be able to hold onto the photo until the end.

TRUE ENDING

» After completing City with the photo, immediately play Plant (Chapter 12). Don't worry, your hand will be empty, but the game will remember your progress. Finish the map as normal.

» Now watch the WHOLE end credits. When you're prompted to choose George or Mr. P, go to Mr. P. As a reward for this, you'll see the True Ending, receive a badge proving you did it, AND get a brand new, completely free skin in the shop: Mr. P's skin!

TEST YOUR ROBLOX SKILLS

JAILBREAK SPOT THE DIFFERENCE

Test your observation! Here's a picture of a prison from Jailbreak, but we've made 10 changes to the bottom image! Can you spot them all?

Read about Jailbreak on page 24 - and then test your skills here!

TEST YOUR ROBLOX SKILLS

JAILBREAK WORDSEARCH

If you read our piece on the brilliant Jailbreak, you might get a headstart with this wordsearch! Hunt the words that might help you break out!

M	U	S	E	U	M	J	P	W	H	C	J	V	D	M	J	A
K	W	G	I	J	T	L	C	H	V	L	E	C	I	L	O	P
B	C	A	S	H	T	R	U	C	K	K	W	K	Q	W	E	A
J	S	N	T	B	Q	V	U	E	N	H	E	E	Z	I	C	R
H	B	O	P	E	S	F	H	N	J	Q	L	V	C	M	G	T
Y	M	S	F	G	R	B	Y	E	V	Y	R	X	F	K	C	M
B	E	I	E	S	B	F	R	G	I	O	Y	M	C	U	E	E
U	L	R	P	V	M	H	A	Z	L	S	S	A	G	A	D	N
C	C	P	O	W	E	R	P	L	A	N	T	Z	A	Y	U	T
M	A	V	I	T	U	S	A	Y	L	X	O	S	B	U	S	S
X	R	G	Z	G	I	T	S	K	P	B	R	X	L	A	E	I
F	G	C	A	R	G	O	S	H	I	P	E	L	E	V	U	G
Y	Q	V	C	E	O	Y	E	X	D	T	X	H	F	G	C	W
J	M	P	W	E	U	E	N	W	W	F	X	O	F	B	S	N
A	O	M	R	O	Y	M	G	T	X	N	V	P	U	P	R	I
I	P	R	I	S	O	N	E	R	C	T	D	C	D	S	E	N
L	O	U	F	T	S	D	R	M	L	F	S	Q	V	S	B	G
B	N	B	N	I	A	R	T	O	G	R	A	C	W	T	B	H
R	B	B	A	E	Z	S	R	H	B	H	Y	X	V	Q	O	P
E	L	K	J	R	D	T	A	U	X	F	B	U	Z	S	R	S
A	D	W	Z	K	K	Y	I	W	B	E	O	W	U	Z	T	T
K	N	A	B	Y	P	E	N	F	N	G	U	N	S	H	O	P

APARTMENTS
BANK
CARGO SHIP
CARGO TRAIN
CASH TRUCK
DUFFEL BAG
GUN SHOP
HEISTS
JAILBREAK
JEWELRY STORE
MUSEUM
PASSENGER TRAIN
PIGGY
POLICE
POWER PLANT
PRISON
PRISONER
ROBBERS
TOMB
WATERFALL

WORMFACE! TIPS!

Meet the Roblox game where you're a big, long, wiggly worm!

EAT FOOD TO GET LONGER

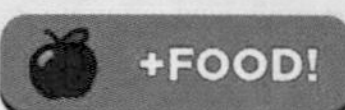

DON'T TOUCH OTHER WORMS!

WHAT DO I NEED TO DO?

Well, it's very simple. You enter the world of Wormface! as a very short worm. Your avatar's face will be on the front of it, and your immediate job is to munch on the food scattered around you, which will help you to become a slightly longer worm! The more you eat, the longer your worm gets. This is all well and good when you're just milling around in the easy communal area, but it gets trickier once you jump into the PvP arena!

This game is good if you've just got five minutes to spare – it would seriously get on your nerves if you were playing it for any longer than that!

DOING BATTLE

There are a few different game modes within Wormface! that you access by slithering over bridges, but some do have access requirements. Understandably, most head for PvP, a battle mode that anybody can get into if their internet connection is quick enough. The idea is to avoid your head hitting another worm. If it does? You lose some of your worm's length. Curses!

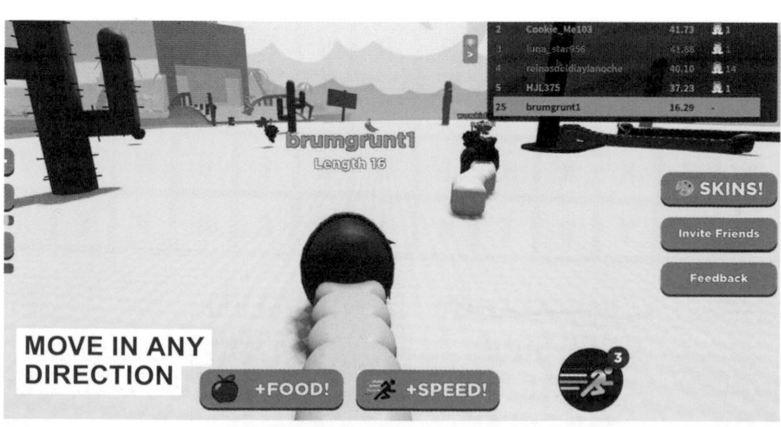

MOVE IN ANY DIRECTION

STARTER TIPS

There are a few things to bear in mind if you're giving Wormface! a go. Remember that you can move in all directions! A good tip can be to press back the controls so you do a

LOOK OUT FOR GEMS

sudden about turn. You're a worm after all, so it's easy to coil yourself and you should use this to your advantage.

Also, not all food is created equal! A slice of cake, for instance, is worth seven times the score of an apple, which means your worm will get longer faster. Foodstuffs to target include burgers and doughnuts (it's not a very healthy game, this one!).

Like many Roblox games, Wormface! tries to get you to buy things. But instead of spending Robux, keep an eye out for the gems that occasionally appear in the playing arena. Pick these up, and you can use them as a form of currency instead – much better than handing over your real money!

GET MUNCHING!

HEAD TO THE PVP ARENA

Finally, you're also given some boosts for your worm, which allow it to move faster for a short period of time. If there are lots of worms in the arena, this can be handy for getting to the good food first! Use these sparingly, though, as you'll have to pay if you want more.

ROBLOX JOKES!

Playing Roblox can get very serious – how about we lighten the mood with some of these rib-ticklers?!??

HOW MUCH IS IT TO PLAY A GAME OF ROBLOX UNDERWATER?

FIVE SQUID!

What did MeepCity say when someone asked what the biggest game in Roblox is?

MEEP! MEEP! MEEP!

WHAT DO YOU CALL A POLICE OFFICER GUARDING A HURDLE?

AN OBBY BOBBY!

Why did the Robloxian have an empty purse?

BECAUSE SHE HAS NOBUX!

WHAT DID THE ROYAL FAMILY PLAY WHEN THEY GOT TO THE TOP OF A HILL?

ROYALE HIGH!

What do you call an obstacle that's big and slimey?

A blobby obby!

Why was there nothing to play on Roblox?

Because someone TookHaven!

WHAT'S THE BEST PLACE IN ROBLOX TO GET SOMETHING TO KEEP YOUR FEET WARM?

SOCKSBURG!

WHICH JOB DO I PICK?

There are six roles in the game, each of which can earn you money!

» CASHIERS take orders by hitting the correct buttons. Easy mode is for beginners, but there's a hard mode if you want more of a challenge!

» COOKS assemble pizzas. Remember, all pizzas have cheese on, so you can make a bunch of cheese pizzas to speed things up – but don't make too many, because they can go cold!

» BOXERS pack the orders for delivery. Try to pack pizzas as soon as they arrive to keep everything organised!

» DELIVERERS take orders to the correct address. Keep track of where pizzas are going, and try to deliver orders that are close together at the same time!

» SUPPLIERS ensure the pizza place has all the ingredients and food it needs to run properly. Remember that to deliver the supplies you need to back in the truck so you can unload it!

» MANAGERS can take the job by sitting in the manager's chair when it's free. This allows you to give out bonuses, send people back to work, vote for bans or give someone the employee of the day award! Bad managers can be voted out, so be fair!

WORK AT A PIZZA PLACE

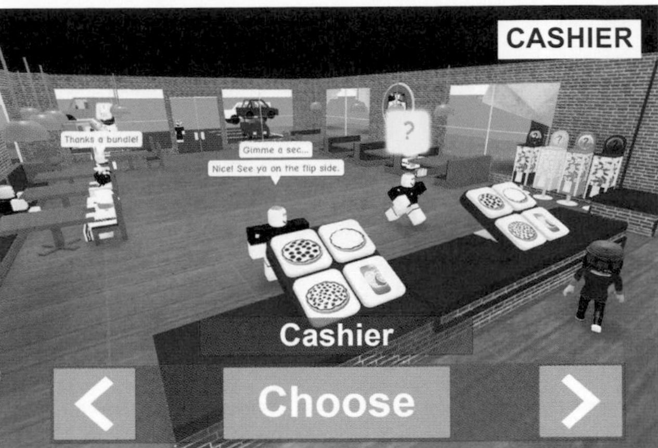

CASHIER

IMPROVING YOUR HOUSE

Houses come in nine sizes, and you can improve your house by earning Moneyz from doing your job well, then upgrading it or buying furniture. You start with a tiny house, and here's how each level improves it:

» Small House (1,200 Moneyz) – More floorspace.

» Medium House (3,700 Moneyz) – Even more floorspace!

» Large House (5,200 Moneyz) – Biggest ground floor possible.

» Two Storey House (14,900 Moneyz) – Adds a second floor and staircase.

» Three Storey House (16,000 Moneyz) – Adds a third floor and staircase.

» Backyard (30,000 Moneyz) – Adds a rear garden to your house.

» Basement (45,000 Moneyz) – Adds a basement level!

» Mansion (200,000 Moneyz) – Improves your house with an extra balcony, space for up to 800 furniture items, custom colours and more! Can be bought for 3,000 Robux.

IMPROVING YOUR HOUSE

MORE TIPS!

You can get videos for your TV by finding another house with a TV and stealing their videos!

Just past the Drive-Thru window, you can see a brick that doesn't look quite right. Jump through it and you'll find a secret hiding place!

You can join the Party Server to show off your house without having to do your job!

The RAREST ROBLOX Toys

Roblox's action figures are hot property – here are the hardest-to-find ones!

PIZZA DELIVERY GUY

From 2017's Work at a Pizza Place Pack, this figure came bundled with the chef, and the popularity of this game means he's hard to find! If you can find an original boxed version, you'll also be able to redeem the Builder Brother's Pizza Chef Hat as an in-game item!

MEME PACK

First released in July 2020, the Roblox Meme Pack brings to life some of the funniest online in-jokes involving Roblox characters and items. It includes hilarious figures, such as thunder1222's Meganoob, the Despacito Spider from Robloxian Highschool and the clown from Fantastic Frontier. You can occasionally still find it on shelves, but it's disappearing fast!

JAILBREAK SWAT UNIT

A vehicle and two-figure set released in the Series 4 toy set, the popularity of this game and the coolness of the toy make it a hard-to-find rarity! The in-game item includes some tactical headgear, but if you can get your hands on this set it's the awesome vehicle you'll enjoy playing with most – there aren't many Roblox vehicle toys to choose from, after all!

TOWER BATTLES: ZED

Another vehicle entry, this one comes from popular zombie-extermination game Tower Battles and takes the form of an awesome robot tank. The ZED is a heavy-firepower vehicle that looks cool and seats one Roblox figure. It also comes with a portable gatling gun as a digital item, so you can have some serious muscle both in and out of the cockpit.

ROYALE HIGH SCHOOL ENCHANTRESS

Is it any surprise that probably the single rarest figure ever made is from Royale High? This one has been seen selling for almost £70, so if you've got one hang onto it! This was the first ever Roblox Royale High toy, and comes with a dorm key and chemistry book. The digital code gets you the Enchantress Tress hair item.

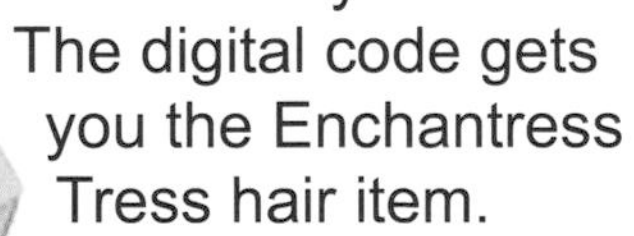

CELEBRITY FASHION FAMOUS

This recent release is flying off the shelves thanks to its tie-in nature and the fact it's based on the popular pageant game, Fashion Famous. It isn't rare yet, but it's sure to be soon – it already costs a lot, which means there are fewer numbers out there to begin with. Pick it up while you can if you like Roblox's fashion games!

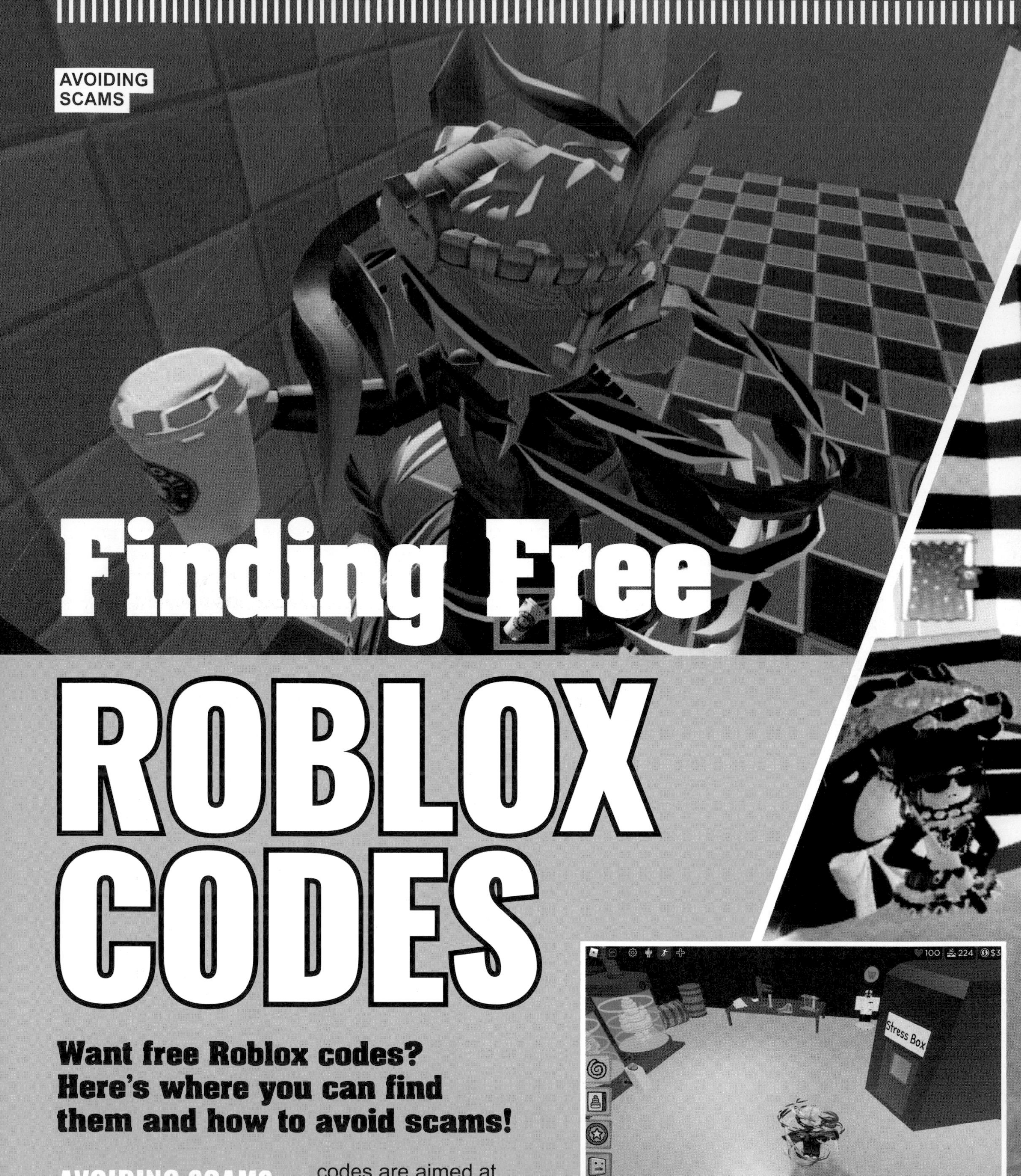

Finding Free ROBLOX CODES

Want free Roblox codes? Here's where you can find them and how to avoid scams!

AVOIDING SCAMS

Remember, these codes won't get you free Robux. The only way to get Robux is by paying for them! Rather, these codes are aimed at specific games and given out by their creators to encourage you to drop in, or they let you get free stuff from the store that isn't available to buy!

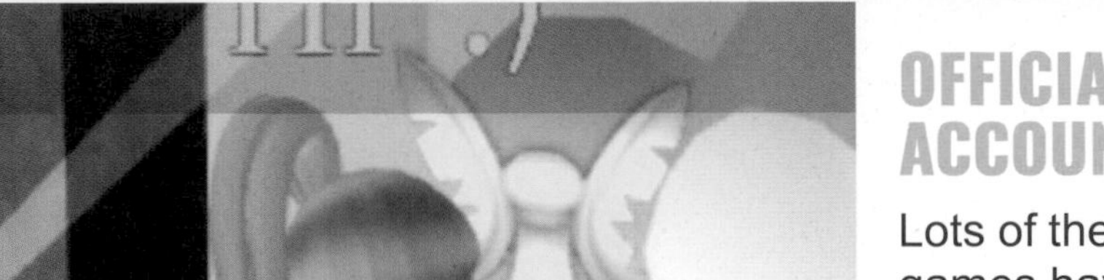

TOYS

REDEEMING CODES

OFFICIAL ACCOUNTS

Lots of the biggest Roblox games have official social media accounts – for example, @PlayAdoptMe on Twitter is the official Adopt Me! account. Official outlets such as these will keep you up to date with in-game events, new updates and releases, connect you with other players and, of course, let you know if any free in-game items are being given away. Ask your grown-up to help you check them out!

POCKET TACTICS

www.pockettactics.com/roblox/promo-codes

This web page combs the internet for free item codes and collects them all here. As an added bonus, it lets you know when they were last updated, so they should always be up to date! There are banner ads on the page, but you don't need to click on anything, and you don't need to pay for anything. A great source of codes!

TOYS

When you buy an official Roblox toy, it should come with a free Roblox digital item code on a slip of paper inside the box. Take care when buying figures, as there are some bootleg figures out there that don't have these codes! Legitimate Roblox toys ALWAYS have a free digital item included in the box.

TWITTER

twitter.com/realrobloxcodes

This Twitter account helpfully tweets any free Roblox codes it verifies, some of which are for the Roblox avatar shop and others that are for in-game items in specific games only. It doesn't update often – just every couple of weeks – but when it does you know these codes are verified and legitimate!

REDEEMING CODES

www.roblox.com/promocodes

If you have a code for Robux that you've bought from a shop, or a free item code for stuff in the shop, you can redeem it using the link above. Again, this is the official link for redeeming codes, and anyone else trying to get you to use their website is probably attempting to trick you. Just like you should keep your password safe, you should never put Roblox codes into any other website! The only exception is for in-game items, which can only be bought by putting the code into the Roblox game once you're already playing it.

BROOKHAVEN Hints & Tips

Here's how to get the most out of one of Roblox's best and most popular role-playing games - Brookhaven!

HOW TO GET A HOUSE

A house serves as the base when you play Brookhaven, and also allows you to spend your in-game money on upgrades. Go up one of the ramps from the town, and you'll find a tonne of vacant lots. You can claim one for yourself and build a house on the site. It doesn't cost anything and you don't need to collect anything to set up your house. Just find an empty lot and you can claim it for free with a choice of houses!

HOW TO GET A JOB

Around the city there are loads of places where you can interact with a desk or counter or some other item to take a job. Just like with housing, simply click on the vacant job and you can

HOW TO ROB THE BANK

get assigned it, with all the responsibilities that entails. Having a job earns you money, allowing you to buy items for yourself and your house. Remember, this is a role-play game, so the better you are at your job the more you'll earn!

HOW TO ROB THE BANK

Go into the cleaners and head to your left, where there's a ramp with a sign that reads 'Do not enter'. Go down the ramp and into the room on the left. Click the hanging light, which opens a trap door to a secret base! Inside this base are some explosives. Grab them, then come back out of the trapdoor. In the next room you'll see a narrow passage on your left, which leads to an air vent in the bank. Follow it round, place an explosive in front of the vault, trigger it, then you'll be able to slip inside and loot the money!

FIND THE SECRET EXPERIMENT ROOM

Enter the hospital. Above the front desk, you'll be able to see a hole in the ceiling to the right. Use a ladder to go up there, and you'll find yourself in a secret abandoned room full of weird operating tables and chairs. What could they have been doing there?!

HIDING AWAY

HIDE IN A GRAVE

In the Brookhaven cemetery, you can fall into the grave two spaces to the left of the open one. Down there you'll find a secret area with some weird spooky sounds not found anywhere else in the game!

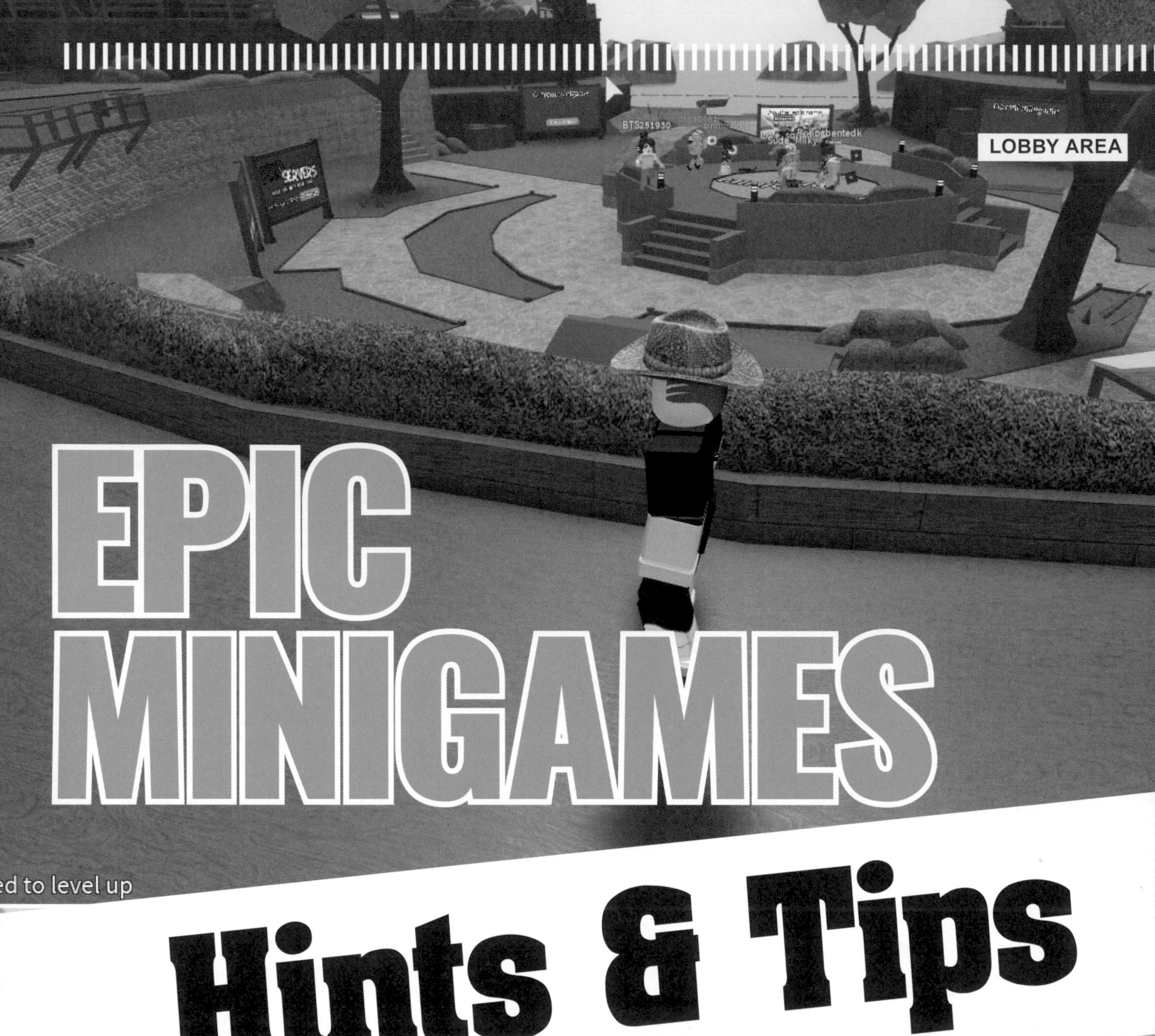

EPIC MINIGAMES

Hints & Tips

If you enjoy playing one game in Roblox, how about almost a hundred of them?!

MINIGAMES

There are – at the time of writing – 89 different games you can play in Epic Minigames, most lasting a minute or so! Usually these games are tests of skill, where a number of players compete on the same field to win a simple objective – to collect the most points, be the first to complete a course, or to survive longest. Some even require everyone playing to work together! They're all great fun, and the speed at which they change means you'll never get bored.

BADGES

When you win certain games, complete them quickly or achieve a high score, you'll win a badge. There are loads to collect, so check them out to find new ways to beat the games. See how many of the harder ones you can get!

LOBBY AREA

In between games, you hang around in the lobby area, which has a bunch of cool stuff to explore, like leaderboards, a water slide and more. There's also one big secret to find...

FIND THE SECRET ROOM

The minigames might not be big enough to hide any secrets, but the hub area is. To access the secret room, you need to do the following:

» Find and click (or tap) the five hats hidden around the map:

- **Fedora:** Behind the rock near the water slide
- **Skull:** On two boxes near the campfire
- **Horned hat:** Hanging on the post by the dock, opposite the slide
- **Mining hat:** Inside the red tent at the campsite
- **Rainbow hat:** Inside the leaderboard building on a tall plant

» Now head up towards the lighthouse/campsite until you see a hatch in the ground. Drop in, and you'll spot a pink door that only opens if all five hats have been clicked. When you enter, you'll receive the 'secret finder' badge!

Points to remember:

» If you leave the game, you'll have to start finding the hats from scratch.

» You can play games in between searching, but you'll probably only have time to find one hat before the next game starts.

» The badge doesn't give you permanent access, so if you quit and come back, the room will be shut again.

PAY A VISIT TO BLOXBURG!

IMPROVE YOUR HOUSE

Live in a fictional city, go to work and build your dream home – it must be Bloxburg!

MOOD

There are four different mood settings in Bloxburg. Use the various items in your house to keep these green, which in turn makes you happy and helps you earn more at work:

Fun Watch TV, dance or read books.

Hunger Use the fridge to cook a meal. Remember, you'll need to pay for the food!

Hygiene Use the shower and sinks in your bathroom.

Energy Sleep in a bed, sit down or drink coffee.

SKILLS

Skills are fun to build up in Bloxburg, and can help you make money faster. You can also earn trophies for completing them. Here are some of the options, with more set to be added to the game:

» Athletic
» Cooking
» Gaming
» Gardening

» Intelligence
» Music
» Painting
» Writing

WORK

There are tonnes of different jobs in Bloxburg, and each one can earn you varying amounts of money. The more you play and get promoted, the more money you'll earn. It's also a good idea to try all the different jobs to improve your stats:

» Seller
» Miner
» Cashier
» Stocker
» Fisherman
» Janitor
» Woodcutter
» Mechanic
» Pizza baker
» Delivery person
» Hairdresser

BUILD MODE

When you move to Bloxburg, you get to pick your own home. There are a few different options, but it's best to start with the free one, which you can always bulldoze later on for money! The other options involve you spending real money, so make sure your grown-up knows exactly what you're planning to do before you click on anything.

Once you've earned some money, you can build your dream home using walls, roofs and floors. You can then decorate it with furniture and other decorative items, and even build a swimming pool or a basement. The game will try to sell you Building Game Passes to build a bigger and better home, but you don't HAVE to buy these!

MORE TIPS!

Use Manage Permissions to allow your friends to be guests in your new home.

Remember to pay your bills through My House.

There are loads of places to visit in Bloxburg, such as the gym, ferris wheel and nightclub.

BUILD A BOAT FOR TREASURE

The ultimate ship-building simulator gives you a chance to test the sea worthiness of your craft – for treasure!

BUILDING A BOAT

You start the game with a small number of building materials that you can piece together, Minecraft style, into a working boat. Once you've created something – and at first it won't look very impressive – you can hit launch to test it on the local river, at which point it will be sent through a series of obstacles with increasing toughness. Every time your boat hits an obstacle, it takes damage and you get a bit closer to falling in...

BETTER LUCK NEXT TIME!

SPEND GOLD

RE-USE DESIGNS

BETTER LUCK NEXT TIME

Touch the water and it's curtains for you. As soon as your boat is no longer keeping you dry, you'll lose health and fail the attempt.

But that's not the end of it, because you'll receive an award based on how well your boat performed, then be given the chance to build a NEW boat, along with new blocks and the ability to buy extras from the in-game shop using the treasure you collected. And next time, maybe things will go a little more smoothly…!

BOAT BUILDING TIPS

» Spend gold quickly – the bigger your boat, the better it will perform.

» Don't build too far back – if you build too close to the rear of your dry dock area, you'll be pushed automatically over to one side when you launch.

» Try to build in a team – that way, you can build a boat quicker, and you'll be able to create something bigger and be more likely to survive than if you do it on your own. Don't worry if you have no one to play with as there are always people to team up with online.

» Place the strongest blocks in the middle, and put the weaker blocks around them for defence.

» Build a roof over your seat if you can – better still, encase the seat in a compartment. This helps you if the boat flips over, because you'll be protected from touching the water.

» You can save the boats you've built before launch, so you can re-use or expand a specific design next time you play. This is ideal if you want to test out some tweaks to your boat to see if you can make it more likely to survive a launch!

» Finally, remember that you don't have to use ALL your blocks. In fact, sometimes it's better to have a smaller, slimmer boat than a massive one. Experiment and see what works best for you!

TEST YOUR ROBLOX SKILLS

TIME TO HIDE

If you're good at Hide & Seek Extreme, you should be able to find your way to the best hiding place in this maze... We've marked it with a sparkle!

WORD SEEKER

Read our Hide & Seek Extreme Tips on page 28, and see if you can find these jumbled-up words – they're all there!

Doom Bats Er Hen

Lit Bit Sun Ya

Pects Ting A Demo

If It Out Yet

Letter Spore

We've told you about the games - now tackle these Roblox puzzles!

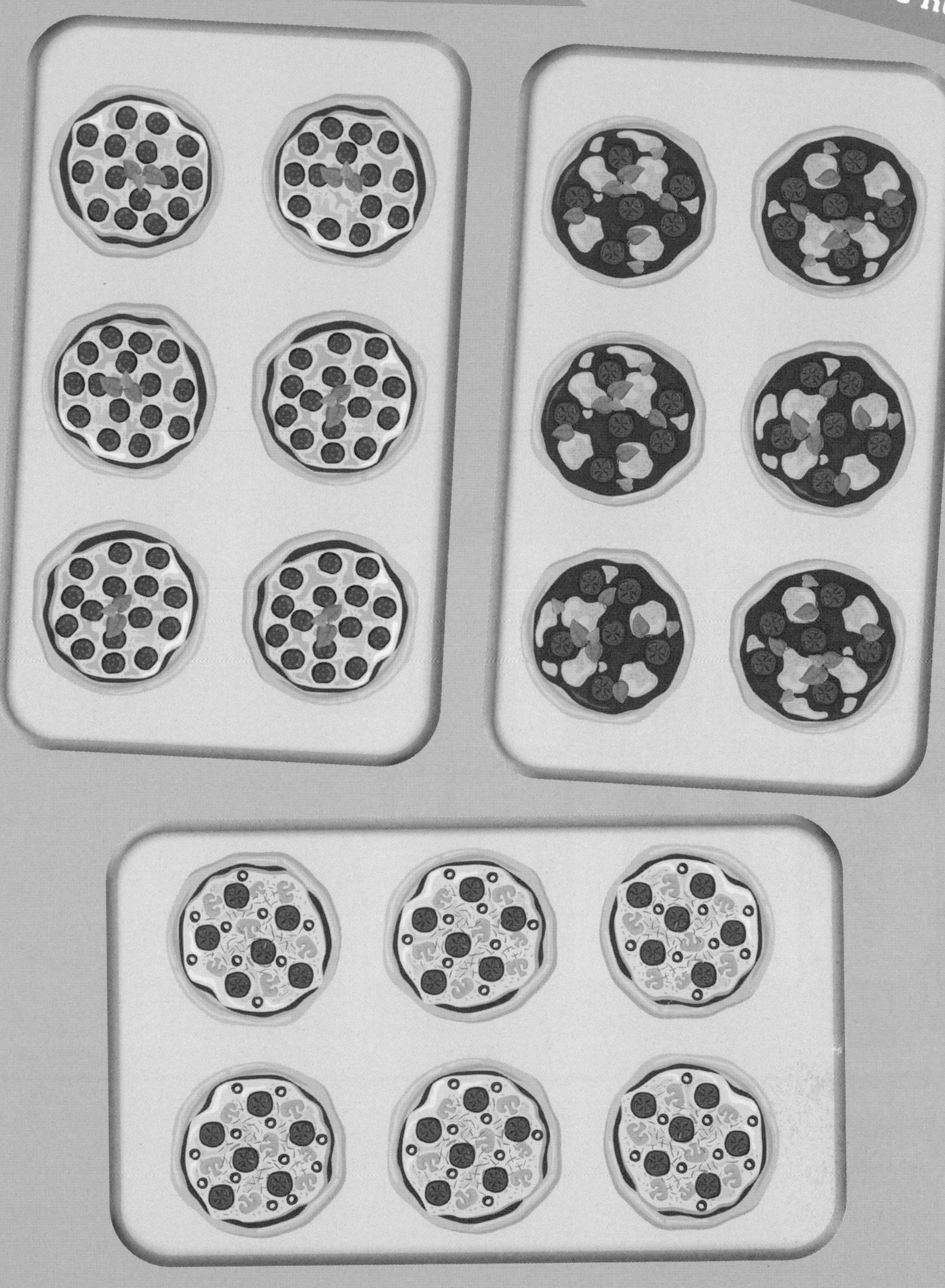

TEST YOUR ROBLOX SKILLS

PIZZA PLACE PARTY

If you want to work at a Pizza Place, you need to know when something's not right... So can you spot which pizza on each tray is the odd one out?

14:19 COMPUTERS LEFT : 4

PLAY AS A TEAM

FLEE THE FACILITY TIPS

Work with friends to hack computers and escape the map before you're caught!

HOW DO I PLAY?

In each round, up to four players will be designated as survivors, and one will be designated as the beast. It's important to work as a team, and the aim is to escape a facility while running away from the beast.

ESCAPING

To escape, you need to hack the computers located around the map.

HACK THE COMPUTERS

ESCAPE FROM THE BEAST

The number of computers changes based on the amount of players. What makes it even more tricky is that once you start to hack a computer, the beast is alerted!

If you're successful, the computer turns green, and if you fail it turns red. But you can keep trying until it turns green!

The beast will be on the lookout, so be careful. It's worth listening closely to the music, as it will speed up when the beast is close by!

Once all the computers are hacked, the doors will open, allowing you to escape and win the round.

RESCUE ME!

THE BEAST WINS!

WHAT HAPPENS IF I'M CAUGHT?

Being caught by the beast doesn't mean the game is over. They'll capture and freeze you, but the other survivors can free and rescue you. But once ALL the survivors are caught, it is mostly definitely game over!

PLAYING THE BEAST

If you're the beast, you start in a different room and have a 15-second delay before you can hunt down the survivors.

You won't be able to crawl through the same openings as the survivors, so it can be harder than it looks to capture them. It will also take you longer to do things like jump, giving the survivors an advantage.

You can win the round by catching all the survivors, but remember that they can try to free themselves, so you need to have your wits about you!

MAPS

There are a few different maps, including Abandoned Prison and Facility_0, and some are more difficult than others. You all need to vote on which map you want to play!

ROBUX

You can use Robux to purchase crates containing different versions of the hammer used by the beast to freeze the survivors. But if you ask us, you really don't need to buy a new hammer!

Climb the GIANT MAN

It's an obby with a difference – and that difference is you're climbing a giant man!

THE GIANT MAN

This game is built by Terry Cavanagh, an Irish game developer living in London who made the awesome games VVVVVV, Super Hexagon and Dicey Dungeons. His Roblox obby, Climb the Giant Man, took a couple of months to build, and it should take around an hour to beat if you play the whole thing. Just look at how tall this man is!

TIMING IS EVERYTHING

When it comes to beating an obby, the best thing you can do is take things slowly. Try to plan where you're going, and make sure you know where you want to land before you hit jump. Lots of the stages in Climb the Giant Man are tough, but everything can be done in a few goes, as long as you take care and don't just run ahead!

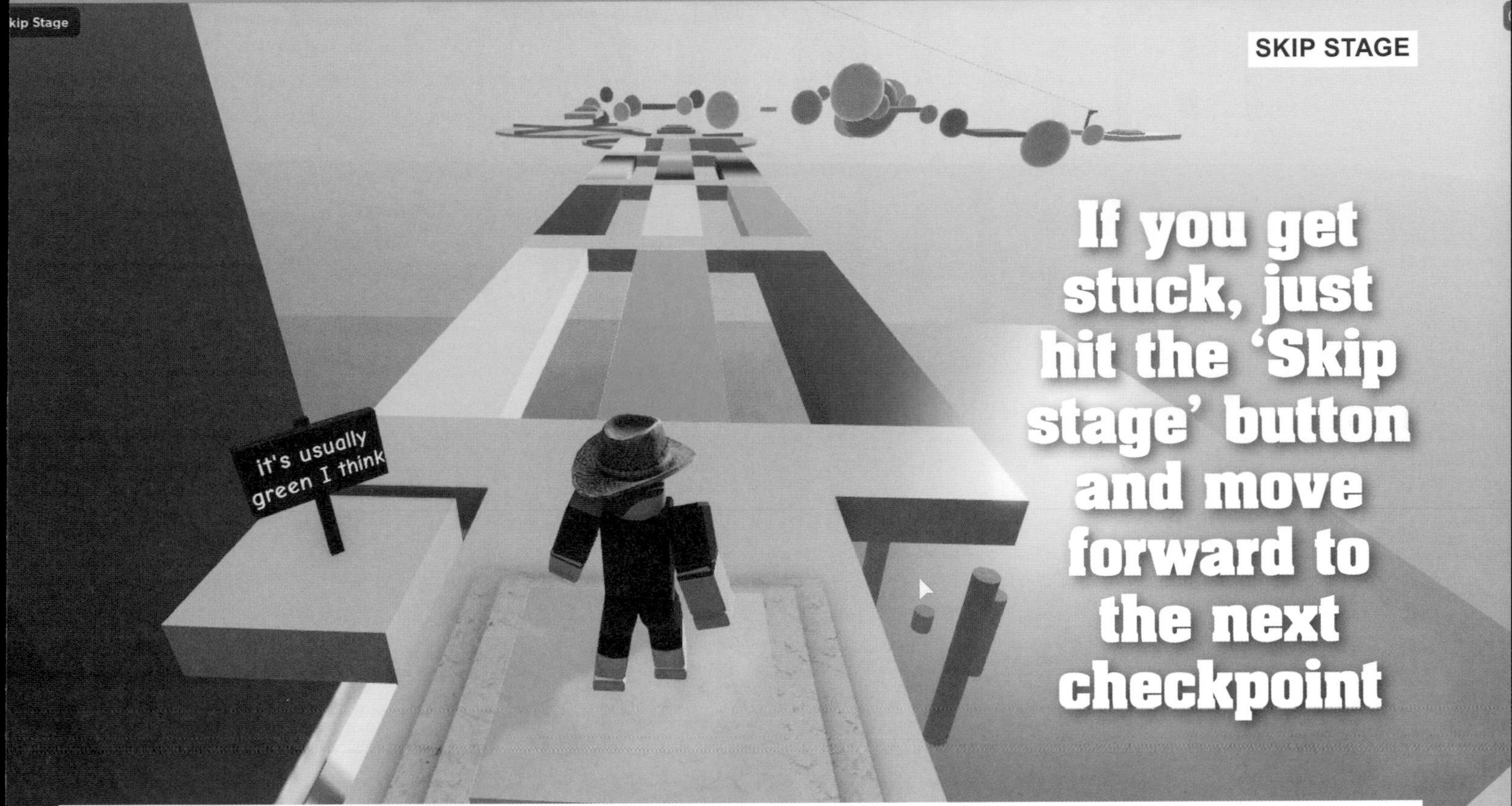

SKIP STAGE

If you get stuck, just hit the 'Skip stage' button and move forward to the next checkpoint

SKIP STAGE

Don't forget, one of the good things about this obby is that if you get stuck, you can just hit the 'Skip stage' button and move forward to the next checkpoint. You don't even have to spend any Robux to do it! Try to complete the challenge without using it, but if you're genuinely stuck, the Skip stage button means the fun doesn't have to end when things get tough.

ENJOY THE FINAL STAGE

When you reach the head of the Giant Man, you'll find a cool rest area where you can enjoy a jacuzzi, paint yourself a different colour and generally have fun – there's even the option to let yourself fly! Once you exit, you'll be able to visit the gift shop before making your way back to the foot of the Giant Man – and then there's only one thing to do...

ENJOY THE FINAL STAGE

ADMIRE THE DETAILS

Hidden around the Giant Man obby are some neat little touches, such as newspapers with articles about the Giant Man and buttons you can press for cool effects. Take time to look around so that, for example, when you reach the top you'll understand exactly WHY you saw so many cars scattered around the ground on your way up...

GRAB A COFFEE

When you finish the course, don't forget to grab a coffee at Starblox! You can head to the rear of the building to sneak into the kitchen and serve yourself a free drink. Now sit by the window, and look out at the Giant Man and everyone attempting to make the ascent. If you can carry a drink all the way up to the gift shop, you'll even earn yourself a badge!

BRILLIANT ROBLOX YouTubers

Roblox is one of the most popular topics on YouTube, with a whole host of channels devoted to it. Here are some of our favourite Roblox YouTubers!

Name: Jelly
Subscribers: 21.7M
Nationality: Dutch
Streaming since: 2014
Roblox games: Sharkbite, Roblox Themepark Tycoon, Flee The Facility, Pizza Place and loads more!

Why are they great?
Jelly has amazing, loud and over-the-top reactions to everything! He's silly, fun and great at the games. He regularly teams up with other YouTubers like iamSanna and Dino to play and stream together.

What else do they play & stream?
Jelly plays lots of games, not just Roblox. Some of his favourites are Minecraft, Fortnite and Among Us.

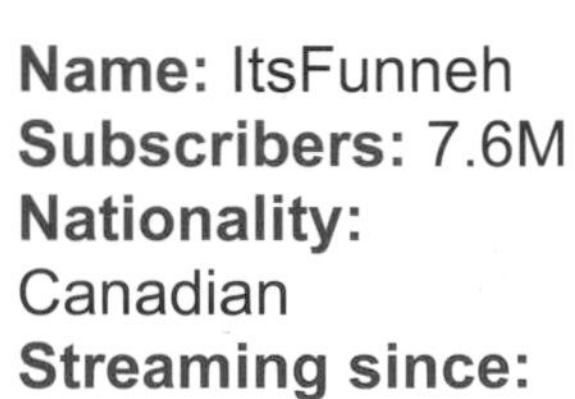

Name: ItsFunneh
Subscribers: 7.6M
Nationality: Canadian
Streaming since: 2011
Roblox games: Hole In The Wall, Rage Runner, Bee Swarm Simulator and Adopt Me!

Why are they great?
Really colourful videos and friendly commentary. Her group of fellow players (The Krew) are always fun, they're not afraid to tease each other, but they also support and help each other through the games. She posts lots of Roblox roleplays, with her video 'First Day at Fairy High School' being her most viewed.

What else do they play & stream?
ItsFunneh also loves Minecraft, minigames, and posts videos of her spending time with The Krew.

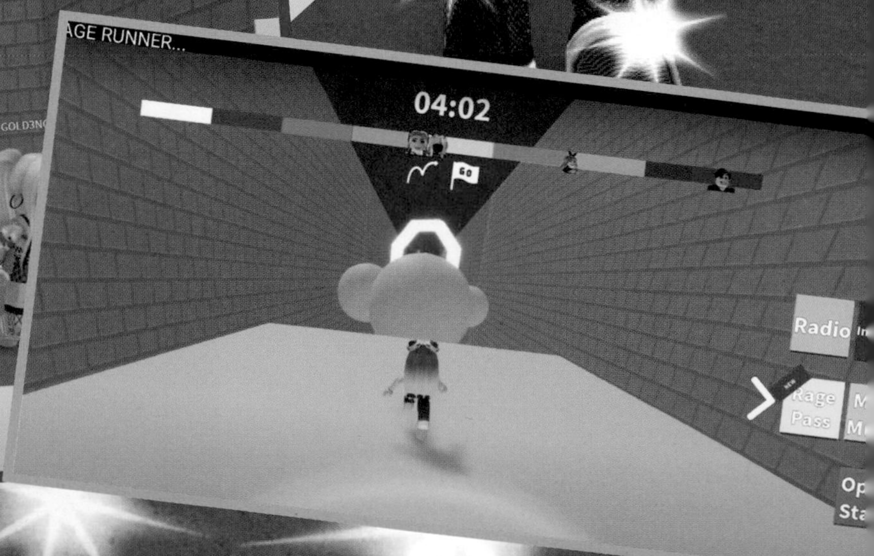

Name: AshleyTheUnicorn
Subscribers: 1.07M
Nationality: American
Streaming since: 2011
Roblox games: Welcome to Bloxburg

Why are they great?
Ashley is one of the best Bloxburg gamers and streamers, and she has some amazing creations from the game. She also does reaction videos to other people's Roblox content like music videos, adding lots of positivity to the Roblox community.

What else do they play & stream?
Ashley's played Fortnite and The Sims 4, but most of her content is on Welcome to Bloxburg.

Name: KonekoKitten
Subscribers: 1.25M
Nationality: American
Streaming since: 2018
Roblox games: Arsenal, Doomspire Brickbattle and different obby games.

Why are they great?
Not only does he create videos of his gameplay with amazing commentary – such as trying out the most difficult obby courses – he also makes great reactionary videos about the Roblox community.

What else do they play & stream?
KonekoKitten has played other games in the past, but his channel is just for Roblox.

Name: FGTeeV
Subscribers: 19.1M
Nationality: American
Streaming since: 2013
Roblox games: Piggy as well as Super Pizza Hero, Adopt Me! and others

Why are they great?
Not just one person, but a whole family of Roblox players! 'Duddy' edits all the videos, playing the games with his family members. The videos from FGTeeV are some of the best edited Roblox videos on YouTube. They're always fun and silly, but also extra creative and look great.

What else do they play & stream?
They play games like Among Us and Bendy and the Ink Machine, but they also post videos of songs and comedy skits they do together.

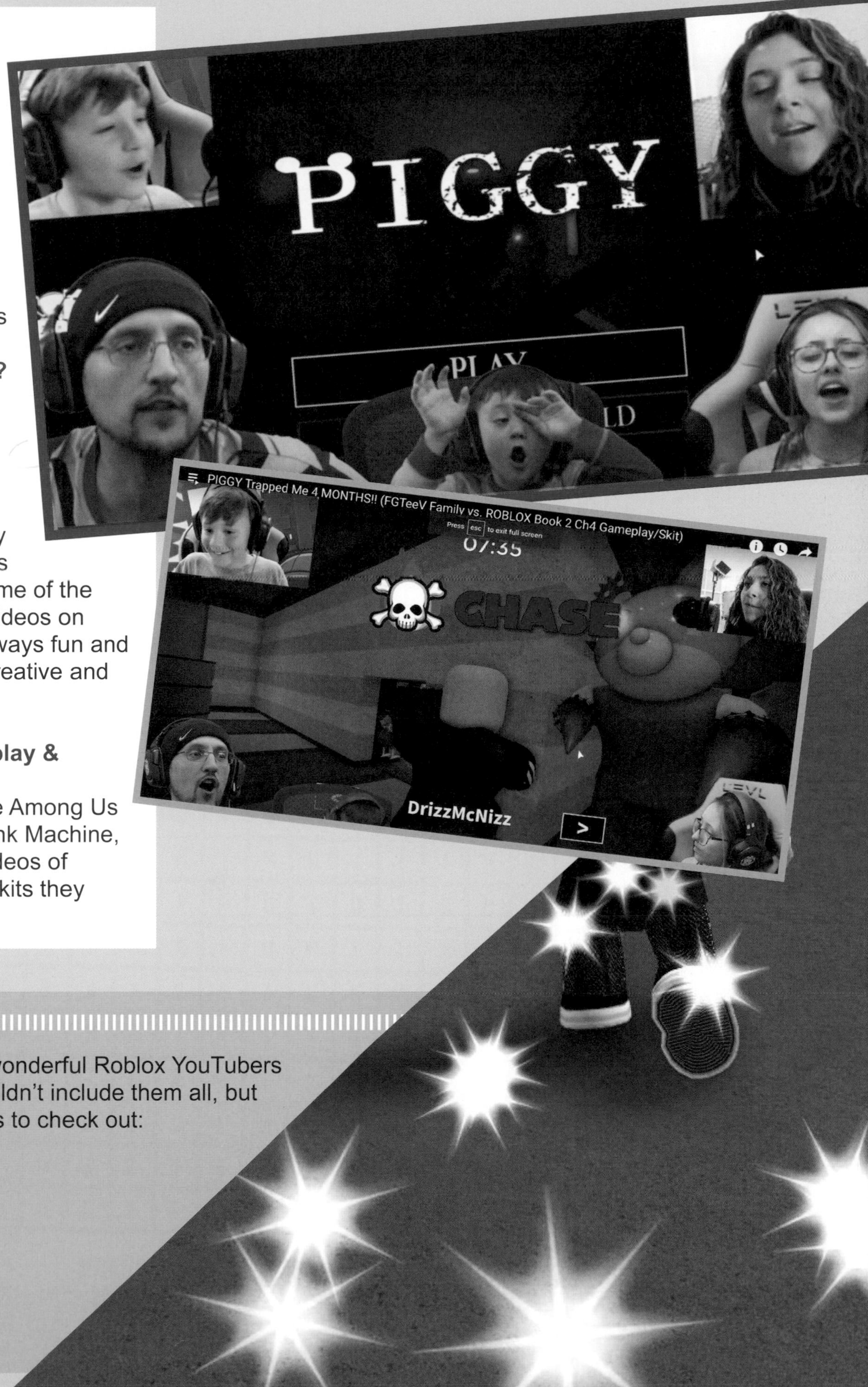

There are so many wonderful Roblox YouTubers out there that we couldn't include them all, but here are some others to check out:

Flamingo
Bigbst4tz2
Sketch
MicroGuardian
iamSanna
MeganPlays
RussoPlays

TEST YOUR ROBLOX SKILLS

MAKE A CAKE WORD HUNT

Somewhere in the grid below are 20 words connected to the Roblox Make A Cake game, and don't forget you can read more about it on page 68!

C	V	Y	U	D	C	G	Y	U	K	C	Z	W	B	P	Y	Q
A	Q	B	M	I	X	I	N	G	S	T	A	T	I	O	N	X
K	U	C	B	N	J	A	D	A	E	W	A	E	R	R	P	M
E	G	R	J	L	O	N	Y	F	P	J	O	J	Y	T	F	E
M	O	U	T	H	S	T	D	E	Q	D	A	R	B	A	A	T
A	X	E	N	S	H	N	R	O	B	Y	S	I	D	L	R	A
C	E	K	Y	J	M	O	N	E	X	R	U	S	B	X	L	L
H	D	I	T	Y	L	O	U	R	D	O	K	H	C	H	Q	T
I	R	U	O	P	B	B	J	U	J	N	H	F	D	E	B	A
N	A	R	X	A	K	D	Z	S	V	Y	E	V	M	A	A	B
E	O	E	W	C	M	G	K	W	I	O	D	L	Z	I	C	L
M	B	S	O	N	X	C	K	V	B	R	I	Q	B	A	K	E
M	R	P	P	H	H	Y	S	E	T	X	C	O	H	L	F	I
D	E	A	C	I	L	L	U	M	I	N	A	T	I	M	O	E
C	D	W	G	B	Z	U	Z	U	G	I	H	L	Q	Z	R	I
H	A	N	V	R	J	J	W	D	J	A	C	O	N	N	S	M
D	E	T	Y	X	M	A	K	E	A	C	A	K	E	X	E	X
C	L	X	C	U	L	R	Y	I	A	Y	M	R	Z	G	C	V
S	P	A	R	K	L	E	S	O	F	M	O	I	C	E	O	H
M	Z	X	L	J	L	S	R	N	Y	U	T	L	N	A	N	Y
T	D	P	D	Z	N	W	E	D	E	T	S	E	G	I	D	X
B	A	T	T	E	R	E	Q	T	Y	Q	N	O	D	U	S	E

ARCADE
BACK FOR SECONDS
BAKE
BATTER
BLENDER
CAKE MACHINE
DIGESTED
EXPLORE
GIANT NOOB
ILLUMINATI
LEADERBOARD
MAKE A CAKE
METAL TABLE
MIXING STATION
MOUTH
PORTAL
RESPAWN
SPARKLES
STOMACH ACID
SWORD

OLD VERSIONS

SECRET SWORD

Hanging on the left of the front wall, inside the giant noob's mouth, is a sword you can grab. Plan your route carefully and you'll be able to snatch it before climbing back out of the noob's mouth. Take care, though – if you fall into the stomach acid, you'll be digested along with the rest of the food and eventually be forced to respawn without anything you've collected.

SECRET SWORD

ILLUMINATI EASTER EGG

To find the illuminati easter egg, sneak behind the blender and look for the face with green sparkles around it. Head through the face and you'll find yourself in a secret room showing the connection between cakes and the Illuminati! You'll also receive a special face that you can get rid of by resetting your character or using the de-cake button.

ILLUMINATI EASTER EGG

PORTAL EASTER EGG

A reference to one of the all-time classic computer games can be found behind the baking station, where there's a portal with sprinkles around it. Enter the room and touch the metal table inside to turn into a metal cake unavailable elsewhere in the game. Again, use the reset or de-cake options to revert to your normal appearance!

ROBLOX STUDIO GUIDE

If you've got access to a PC, the free Roblox Studio software allows you to build your own games, items and more!

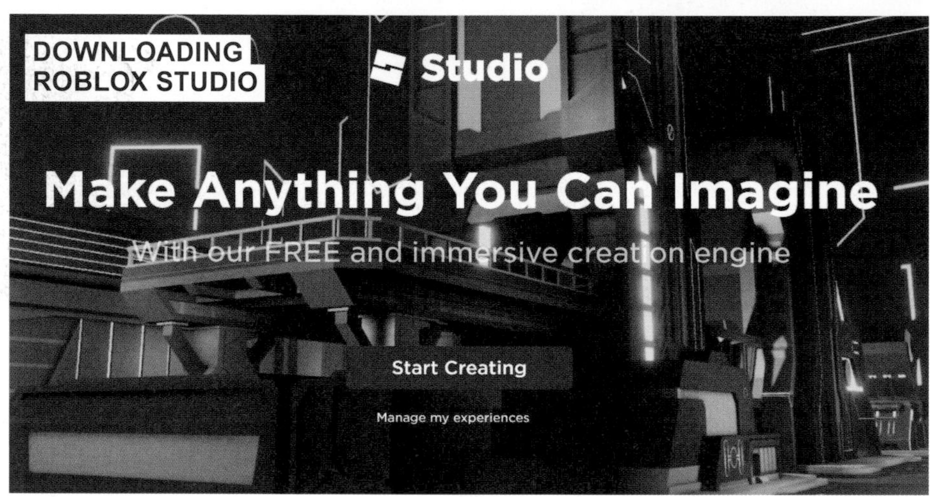

DOWNLOADING ROBLOX STUDIO

DOWNLOADING ROBLOX STUDIO

Roblox Studio is available for free on Windows and MacOS – you just have to download it! You can get it from the official site by visiting **www.roblox.com/create** and following the instructions. Note that it can't be downloaded for mobile platforms like iOS and Android – this is purely for desktop and laptop systems!

Once you've downloaded the executable, just run it and follow the instructions. The downloads aren't very big and the software itself has very low requirements. As long as you can run Roblox, your system should be able to run Roblox Studio.

TEMPLATES

When you launch the Studio software, you'll be given a selection of templates. You can either start with a completely empty baseplate to begin creating on, or select one of the themed baseplates, which come with pre-built items and environments. If, for example, you wanted to build an obby, you could select the 'Obby' template, which comes with a basic course that you can modify and copy!

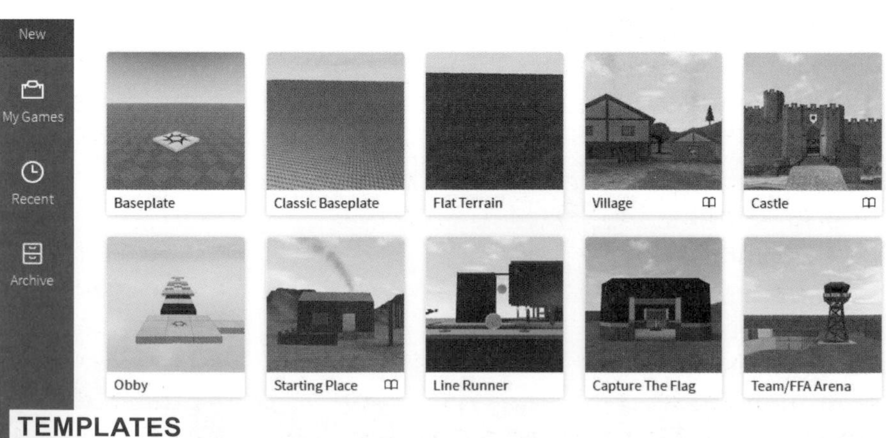

TEMPLATES

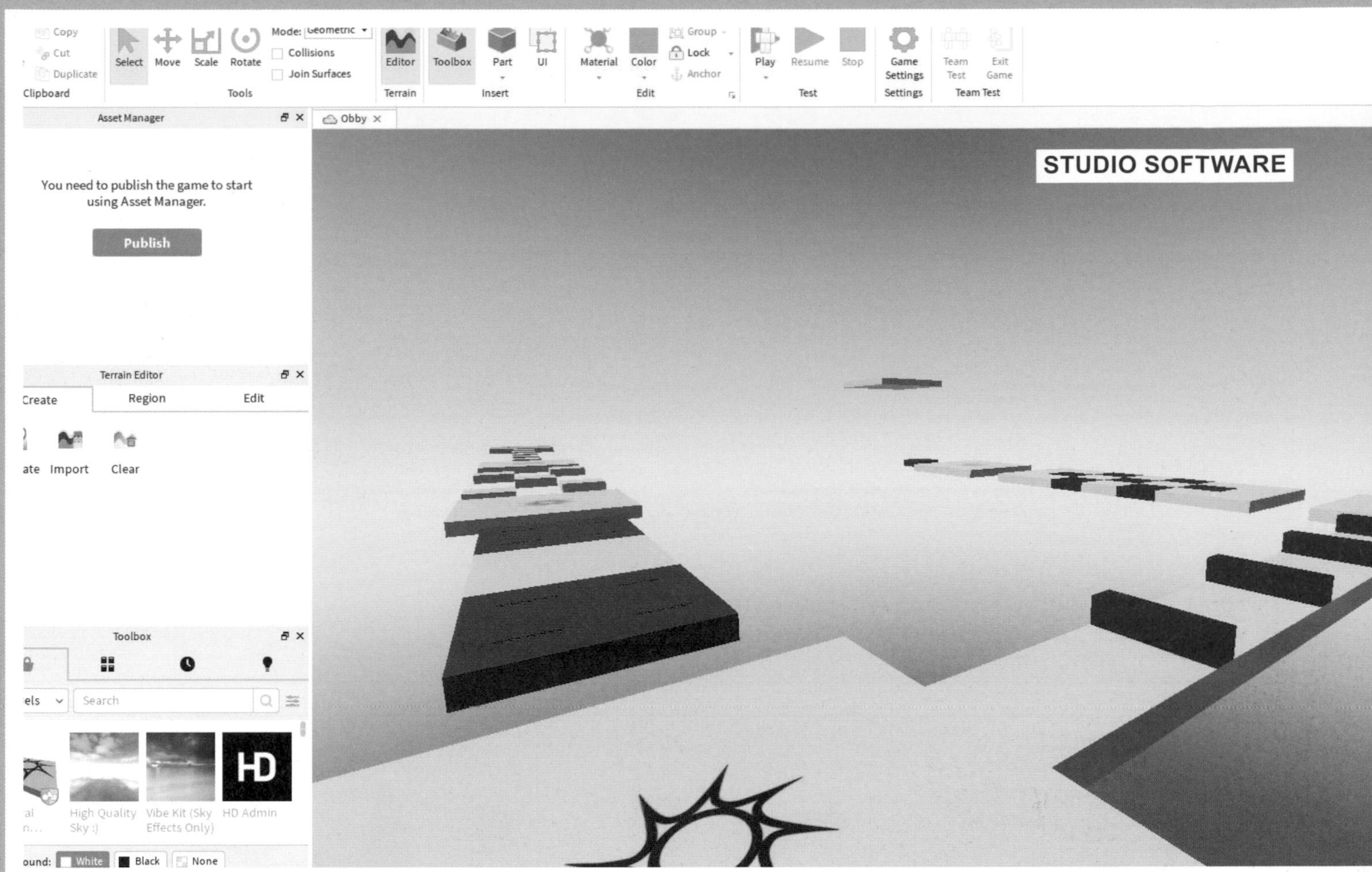

The Studio software is made up of three main sections:

THE RIBBON

Located at the top of the interface, the Ribbon allows you to choose how you interact with the items you're building. The Selection tool lets you pick something in your building area, while Move, Scale and Rotate allow you to manipulate the selected item. You can use the 'Home' ribbon to change the colour and material of your selection, or add new items using the 'Part' button. You can also test out what you've built by hitting 'Play'. Expanded versions of these options are available in the Model, Test, View and Plugin ribbons.

TOOLBOXES

On the left and right of the default layout, you'll find Toolboxes that allow you to edit assets, dive into their specific properties, and select models from the online catalogues of free models. This stuff is all pretty complicated, so don't feel intimidated if you can't understand it straight away. Play with the pre-built items and you'll start to see how it all links together.

Play with the pre-built items and you'll start to see how it all links together

THE PLAY WINDOW

Like a mini version of Roblox, the play window allows you to move the camera around using the mouse and keyboard, as well as directly manipulate items in your world. The right mouse button turns the camera, the mouse wheel zooms it in and out, and the WASD keys allow you to move it.

TERRAIN EDITOR

TOOLBOX

TERRAIN EDITOR

Here you can add or remove the terrain. You can also generate a semi-randomised terrain (a bit like Minecraft!), which you can use as the basis for your world in future. Try it out, but on a blank build so you don't risk messing up something you've already made! Select the features you want to see, then hit the 'Generate' button in the Terrain Editor to end up with something similar to the screenshot! You can then use the Region and Edit tools to fine tune what's there, by sculpting the landscape, raising or lowering the sea level, or changing the texture of the land.

TOOLBOX

While you CAN make everything from scratch, one of the great things about the Roblox community is that lots of stuff has already been built for you. In the Toolbox, you can select from a massive number of items in the marketplace to download and use in your world. While some of these items need to be paid for with Robux if you want to use them, a large number are free, so have a look around and choose things relevant to your build!

EXPLORER

In the top right of the Studio, you'll find the Explorer, which lets you interact with every object in your world by name, as well as view some of the properties of the world itself. For instance, every object will appear within the 'Workspace' view – we added a Sakura tree, which is made from a group of leaves, a tree trunk and falling leaves. Elsewhere we can change the player properties and the lighting effects for our world.

To begin with, you shouldn't need to edit too much, but it's good to get into the habit of renaming new objects and any parts you add, so you can keep track of them. That way, you can select them even if you can't see them in your world!

PROPERTIES

This is one of the most important tools in the Studio as it allows you to see and edit the properties of a selected object. Here we've selected the SpawnLocation object, and you can see that its properties allow us to change its appearance, fine tune some of its data, or even move it by editing its positional data directly without any need to use the transform tools, which allows for greater precision. Further down, you can select the way it interacts with the player and any other special properties. Get used to editing these – they're very powerful but well worth learning! Once you've mastered this, you're well on the way to building your own worlds!

ANSWERS

JAILBREAK p36-37

SPOT THE DIFFERENCE & WORDSEARCH

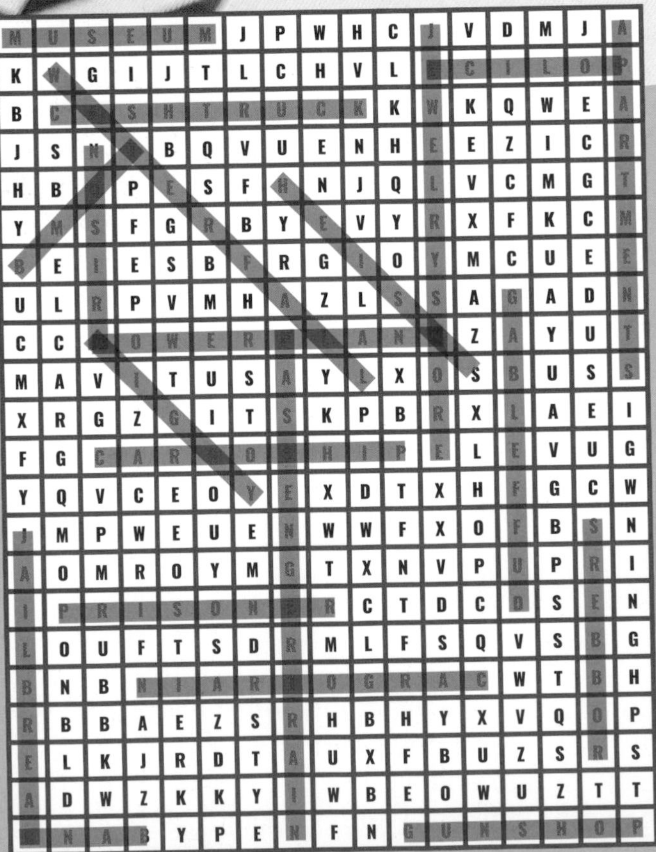

TIME TO HIDE p56

MAZE PUZZLE

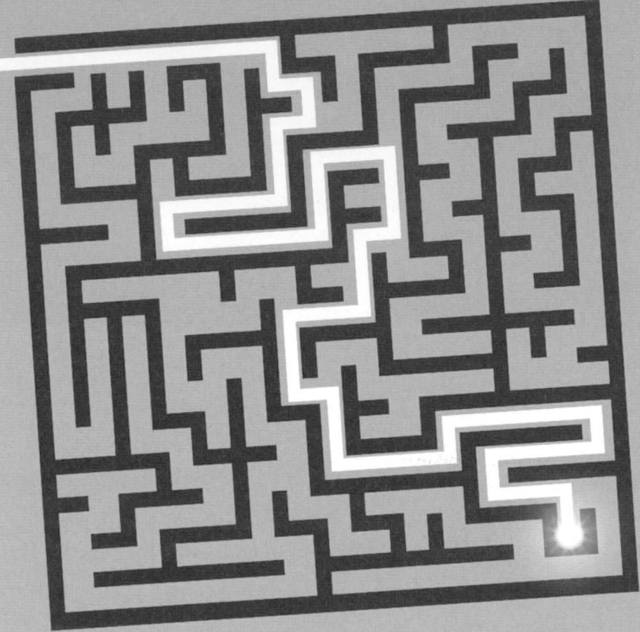

WORD SEEKER p56

Ethan's Bedroom

Stun Ability

Yeti outfit

Spectating Mode

Teleporters

PIZZA PLACE PARTY

p57

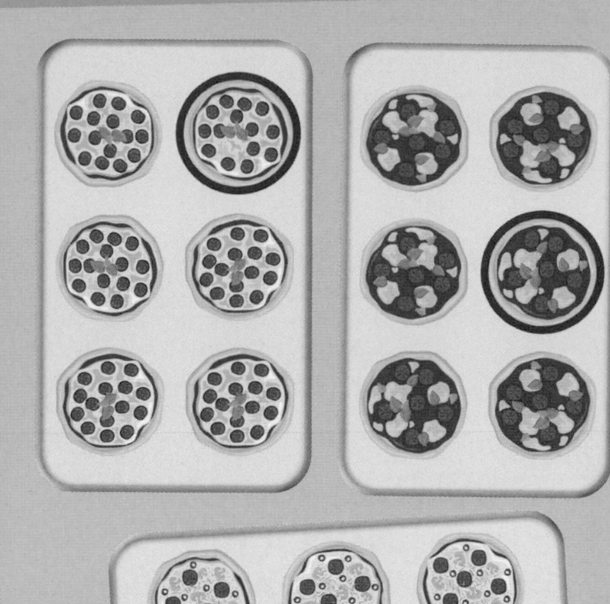

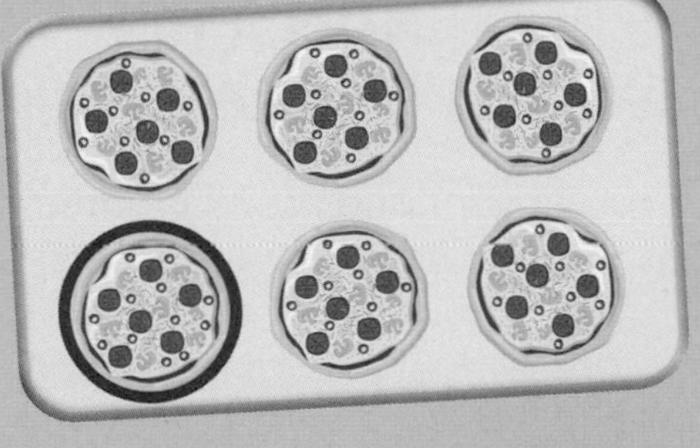

MAKE THE CAKE

p66-67

SPOT THE DIFFERENCE & WORDSEARCH

C	V	Y	U	D	C	G	Y	U	K	C	Z	W	B	P	Y	Q
A	Q	B	M	I	X	I	N	G	S	T	A	T	I	O	N	X
K	U	C	B	N	J	A	D	A	E	W	A	E	R	R	P	M
E	G	R	J	L	O	N	Y	F	P	J	O	J	Y	T	F	E
M	O	U	T	H	S	T	D	E	Q	D	A	R	B	A	A	T
A	X	E	N	S	H	N	D	O	B	Y	S	I	D	L	R	A
C	E	K	Y	J	M	O	N	E	X	R	U	S	B	X	L	L
H	D	I	T	Y	L	O	U	R	D	O	K	H	C	H	Q	T
I	R	U	O	P	B	B	J	U	J	N	H	F	D	E	B	A
N	A	R	X	A	K	D	Z	S	V	Y	E	V	M	A	A	B
E	O	E	W	C	M	G	K	W	I	O	D	L	Z	I	C	L
M	B	S	O	N	X	C	K	V	B	R	I	Q	B	A	K	E
M	R	P	P	H	H	Y	S	E	T	X	C	O	H	L	F	I
D	E	A	C	I	L	L	U	M	I	N	A	T	I	M	O	E
C	D	W	G	B	Z	U	Z	U	G	I	H	L	Q	Z	R	I
H	A	N	V	R	J	J	W	D	J	A	C	O	N	N	S	M
D	E	T	Y	X	M	A	K	E	A	C	A	K	E	X	E	X
C	L	X	C	U	L	R	Y	I	A	Y	M	R	Z	G	C	V
S	P	A	R	K	L	E	S	O	F	M	O	I	C	E	O	H
M	Z	X	L	J	L	S	R	N	Y	U	T	L	N	A	N	Y
T	D	P	D	Z	N	W	E	D	E	T	S	E	G	I	D	X
B	A	T	T	E	R	E	Q	T	Y	Q	N	O	D	U	S	E

HOW WELL DID YOU DO?

PLAY SAFE

Roblox is lots of fun, with a very active online community, but it's worth following some basic tips to make sure you can enjoy it safely.

PROTECT YOUR ACCOUNT WITH A PIN

Delve into Roblox's settings, and you can add a four-digit PIN to lock your account and prevent others from altering passwords, settings and your email address. That way, you can set restrictions without anyone being able to reverse them.

DECIDE WHO CAN MESSAGE YOU

Don't allow strangers to contact you in Roblox; only allow people you know personally. Open the Settings and choose 'Privacy' from the list of options. You'll then be able to choose 'Friends' from the list. Alternatively, for full safety, you could even select 'No One'.

ENTER YOUR TRUE DATE OF BIRTH AT REGISTRATION

It's vital that you enter a true date of birth when registering, particularly the year the account holder was born. Roblox determines which words and phrases can be used depending on a user's age. It means younger plays can be protected from inappropriate language.

LET ROBLOX'S ADMINS SELECT THE GAMES

Setting a true date of birth won't prevent anyone under the age of 13 accessing any games they wish. To restrict material, consider applying Account Restrictions. This will only allow games from a pre-approved list chosen by Roblox.

Report anything that doesn't feel right

Anything that violates Roblox's terms and conditions should be reported. Click the Flag icon next to a user's name if they're associated with a chat, private message, game or anything else that leaves you feeling uncomfortable, and the person will be brought to the attention of the moderator.

Password-protect credit cards!

It's very easy to rack up a real-life bill, because Robux – the in-game currency – can be purchased using real money. Ensure everyone is aware of the dangers of carefree spending, and pop your financial details behind a password for peace of mind. In-game transactions can also be turned off.

Play together

You don't all have to be in separate rooms if you're playing Roblox in the same house. Try sitting together and talking to each other – and be sure to talk about things that don't seem right.

CHECK THE HISTORY

Grown-ups: don't feel like you're snooping! It's perfectly fine to monitor the activity on a Roblox account by checking out friends and followers, looking at the transaction history, and having a read of any messages and chats. Have a look at the games that are being played too.

Golden rule

Roblox is brilliant fun and there's so much to enjoy, but if ever something makes you feel uncomfortable or just doesn't feel right, make sure you tell your grown-up.

Bullying and grooming can and does happen on Roblox. Never reveal your real name to anyone. Never give out your address. Never meet with anyone you don't know outside of the game. And kids: never feel afraid of telling somebody if you feel uncomfortable.

After all that Roblox-ing, it's time to head home and put our feet up! After we've redecorated our home in Bloxburg, of course! Thanks for reading!